First World War
and Army of Occupation
War Diary
France, Belgium and Germany

37 DIVISION
Divisional Troops
Royal Army Veterinary Corps
28 Mobile Veterinary Section
28 April 1915 - 31 March 1919

WO95/2526/4

The Naval & Military Press Ltd
www.nmarchive.com
Published in association with The National Archives

Published by

The Naval & Military Press Ltd

Unit 10 Ridgewood Industrial Park,

Uckfield, East Sussex,

TN22 5QE England

Tel: +44 (0) 1825 749494

www.naval-military-press.com

www.nmarchive.com

This diary has been reprinted in facsimile from the original. Any imperfections are inevitably reproduced and the quality may fall short of modern type and cartographic standards.

Contents

Document type	Place/Title	Date From	Date To
Heading	WO95/2526/4 Apr 1915-Mar 1919 28th Mob Vet. Sect		
Heading	37th Division 28th Mob. Vety Section Apl 1915-Mar 1919		
Heading	37th Division 28th Mobile Vet. Sect Vol I 1915 Apl-1915 Sep		
War Diary			
War Diary		28/04/1915	29/04/1915
War Diary	Tidworth	30/04/1915	15/05/1915
War Diary	Tidworth Pennings	16/05/1915	17/06/1915
War Diary	Tidworth	02/07/1915	03/07/1915
War Diary	Tidworth	04/07/1915	31/07/1915
War Diary	Havre	01/08/1915	02/08/1915
War Diary	Tilques	03/08/1915	03/08/1915
War Diary	Renescure	04/08/1915	04/08/1915
War Diary	Caestre	05/08/1915	06/08/1915
War Diary	Fletre	07/08/1915	27/08/1915
War Diary	Authieul	28/08/1915	05/09/1915
War Diary	Mondecourt	06/09/1915	08/09/1915
War Diary	Authieul	09/09/1915	11/09/1915
War Diary	Mondecourt	12/09/1915	30/09/1915
Heading	37th Division 28th Mob. Vet. Sect. Vol 2 Oct 15		
War Diary	Mondicourt	01/10/1915	31/10/1915
Heading	37th Division 28th Mob. Vet. Sect Vol. 3 H.Q. 37th Division. A.D.M.S. Vol. 4 Nov. 15 Dec. 15		
War Diary	Mondicourt	01/11/1915	31/12/1915
Heading	28th Mob. Vet. Sect. Vol. 4		
War Diary	Mondicourt	01/01/1916	31/01/1916
War Diary	28th Mob. Vet. Sect. Vol. 5		
War Diary	Mondicourt	01/02/1916	03/02/1916
War Diary	Grincourt	04/02/1916	29/02/1916
Heading	28 MV Sec Vol 6		
War Diary	Grincourt	01/03/1916	19/03/1916
War Diary	Grouches	20/03/1916	02/05/1916
War Diary	Grincourt	02/05/1916	07/05/1916
War Diary	Soncamp	08/05/1916	03/07/1916
War Diary	Grincourt	04/07/1916	15/07/1916
War Diary	Brouilly	26/07/1916	26/07/1916
War Diary	Caucourt	17/07/1916	21/07/1916
War Diary	Hermin	22/07/1916	22/07/1916
War Diary	Beugin	22/07/1916	28/07/1916
War Diary	Fresnicourt	28/07/1916	16/08/1916
War Diary	Labuissiere	16/08/1916	27/08/1916
War Diary	Bruay	27/08/1916	31/08/1916
Heading	War Diary Sept 1916 28th Mob. Vet. Sector 37th Div Vol 12		
War Diary	Labuissiere	01/09/1916	30/09/1916
War Diary	Barlin	21/09/1916	18/10/1916
War Diary	Marest	18/10/1916	20/10/1916
War Diary	Ostreville	21/10/1916	21/10/1916
War Diary	Etree-Wamin	22/10/1916	22/10/1916

War Diary	Orville	23/10/1916	25/10/1916
War Diary	Marieux	26/10/1916	15/11/1916
War Diary	Hedauville	16/11/1916	25/11/1916
War Diary	Marieux	26/11/1916	30/11/1916
Miscellaneous	37th Divn. "A"	31/12/1916	31/12/1916
War Diary	Marieux	01/12/1916	03/12/1916
War Diary	Arqueves	04/12/1916	14/12/1916
War Diary	Fohen-Le-Grand	15/12/1916	15/12/1916
War Diary	Flers.	16/12/1916	16/12/1916
War Diary	Monchiet Cayeux	17/02/1916	17/02/1916
War Diary	Norrent Fontes	18/12/1916	18/12/1916
War Diary	St. Venant	19/12/1916	21/12/1916
War Diary	Lestrem	22/12/1916	25/12/1916
War Diary	Fosse	26/12/1916	31/12/1916
Heading	War Diary 28 Mob Net Sect Jany 1917 Vol 16		
Miscellaneous	To 37th Division "A"		
War Diary	Fosse	01/01/1917	09/01/1917
War Diary	La Fosse	10/01/1917	31/01/1917
Miscellaneous	To 37th Division "A"	01/03/1917	01/03/1917
War Diary	La Fosse	01/02/1917	13/02/1917
War Diary	Drouvin	14/02/1917	28/02/1917
Heading	War Diary 28th Mob. Vet. Section Vol 18 Mar. 1917		
Miscellaneous	To 37 Division A.	31/03/1917	31/03/1917
War Diary	Drouvin	01/03/1917	03/03/1917
War Diary	Norrent-Fontes.	04/03/1917	08/03/1917
War Diary	Rocourt.	09/03/1917	20/03/1917
War Diary	Rocourt St. Laurent.	21/03/1917	31/03/1917
Miscellaneous	DAG Base 37th Div 97	25/05/1917	25/05/1917
War Diary	Rocourt St. Laurent	01/04/1917	04/04/1917
War Diary	Duisans	05/04/1917	13/04/1917
War Diary	Ligneroeul	14/04/1917	14/04/1917
War Diary	Lignereuil	15/04/1917	20/04/1917
War Diary	Etrun	21/04/1917	30/04/1917
Miscellaneous	To 37 Division A.	01/06/1917	01/06/1917
War Diary	Lignereuil	01/05/1917	17/05/1917
War Diary	Warlus	18/05/1917	20/05/1917
War Diary	Arras	21/05/1917	31/05/1917
Heading	War Diary 28th Mob. Vet Section June 1917 Vol 21		
War Diary	Arras	01/06/1917	02/06/1917
War Diary	Lignereuil	03/06/1917	06/06/1917
War Diary	Valhuon	07/06/1917	08/06/1917
War Diary	Lugy	09/06/1917	23/06/1917
War Diary	Steenbecque	24/06/1917	24/06/1917
War Diary	Locre	25/06/1917	30/06/1917
Heading	War Diary 28 Mob Vet Section July 1917 Vol 22		
Miscellaneous	37th Division "Q"	01/08/1917	01/08/1917
War Diary	Locre	01/07/1917	06/07/1917
War Diary	Dranoutre	07/07/1919	31/07/1919
Heading	War Diary 28 Mob Vet Sec Aug 1917 Vol 23		
War Diary	Dranoutre	01/08/1917	08/08/1917
War Diary	Locre	09/08/1917	31/08/1917
Heading	War Diary 28 Mob Vet Section Sept 1917 Vol 24		
Miscellaneous	20/37 Division "A"	01/10/1917	01/10/1917
War Diary	Locre	01/09/1917	09/09/1917
War Diary	St Jans Capel	10/09/1917	12/09/1917
War Diary	St. Jans. Capel	13/01/1917	29/01/1917

War Diary	La Clytte	30/09/1917	30/09/1917
Heading	War Diary 28 Mob Vet Section Oct 1917 Vol 25		
Miscellaneous	To 37th Division "Q"	02/11/1917	02/11/1917
War Diary	La Clytte	01/10/1917	08/10/1917
War Diary	Scherpenburg	09/10/1917	15/10/1917
War Diary	St Jean Capel	16/10/1917	25/10/1917
War Diary	Schaexken	26/10/1917	31/10/1917
Miscellaneous	37th Divn. "Q"	04/12/1917	04/12/1917
War Diary	Schaexken	01/11/1917	10/11/1917
War Diary	Locre	11/10/1917	27/11/1917
War Diary	Laclytte	28/11/1917	14/12/1917
War Diary	Locre	15/12/1917	23/12/1917
War Diary	La Clytte	24/12/1917	14/01/1918
War Diary	Racquinghem	15/01/1918	16/01/1918
War Diary	Westoutre	17/02/1918	27/02/1918
Miscellaneous	To 37th Divn "A"	01/04/1918	01/04/1918
War Diary	Westoutre	01/03/1918	27/03/1918
War Diary	Godsveeldt	28/03/1917	29/03/1917
War Diary	Toutencourt	30/03/1917	30/03/1917
War Diary	Famechon	31/03/1918	31/03/1918
Miscellaneous	To 37th Division "A"	02/05/1918	02/05/1918
War Diary	Famechon	01/04/1918	12/04/1918
War Diary	St Leger. L'Authie	13/04/1918	19/04/1918
War Diary	Authie	20/04/1918	04/06/1918
War Diary	Wargnies	05/06/1916	05/06/1916
War Diary	Breilly	06/06/1918	10/06/1918
War Diary	Plachy-Bunyon	11/06/1918	20/06/1918
War Diary	Flesselles	21/06/1918	21/06/1918
War Diary	Terramasil	22/06/1918	22/06/1918
War Diary	Pas	23/06/1918	31/07/1918
War Diary	Pas En Artois	01/08/1918	26/08/1918
War Diary	Fonquevillers	27/08/1918	27/08/1918
War Diary	Logeast Wood	28/08/1918	03/09/1918
War Diary	Avesnes-Les-Bapaume	04/09/1918	08/09/1918
War Diary	Favreuil	09/09/1918	11/09/1918
War Diary	Fremicourt	12/09/1918	20/09/1918
War Diary	Warlencourt Eaucourt	21/09/1918	29/09/1918
War Diary	Villers-Au-Flos	29/09/1918	30/09/1918
War Diary	Neuville	30/09/1918	06/10/1918
War Diary	Gouzeacourt	06/10/1918	08/10/1918
War Diary	Vauchelles	09/10/1918	09/10/1918
War Diary	Chateau Biseux	10/10/1918	13/10/1918
War Diary	Ligny	14/10/1918	22/10/1918
War Diary	Caudry	23/10/1918	23/10/1918
War Diary	Beaurain	24/10/1918	31/10/1918
War Diary	Beaurain	01/11/1918	05/11/1918
War Diary	Louvignies	06/11/1918	18/11/1918
War Diary	Caudry	12/11/1918	19/11/1918
War Diary	Caudry	01/12/1918	01/12/1918
War Diary	Gommegnies	02/12/1918	14/12/1918
War Diary	Sous Le Bois	15/12/1918	17/12/1918
War Diary	Binche	18/12/1918	19/12/1918
War Diary	Gosselies	20/12/1918	20/12/1918
War Diary	Gosselies	01/01/1919	31/03/1919

WO 95 2526/4

Apr 1915 - Mar 1919

28th Mob Vet. Sect

37TH DIVISION

28TH MOB. VETY SECTION

APL ~~AUG~~ 1915-MAR 1919

37th Division

121/7051

28th Mobile Vet: Sect:

Vol I

Aug & Sept 15

Mar '19

1915 APL - 1915 SEP

Paget. 24.4.15 to 31.3.17.
1.5.17 to 31.3.18

Instructions regarding War Diaries and Intelligence Summaries are contained in F. S. Regs., Part II. and the Staff Manual respectively. Title pages will be [illegible]ed in manuscript.

WAR DIARY
or
~~INTELLIGENCE SUMMARY.~~
(Erase heading not required.)

Army Form C. 2118.

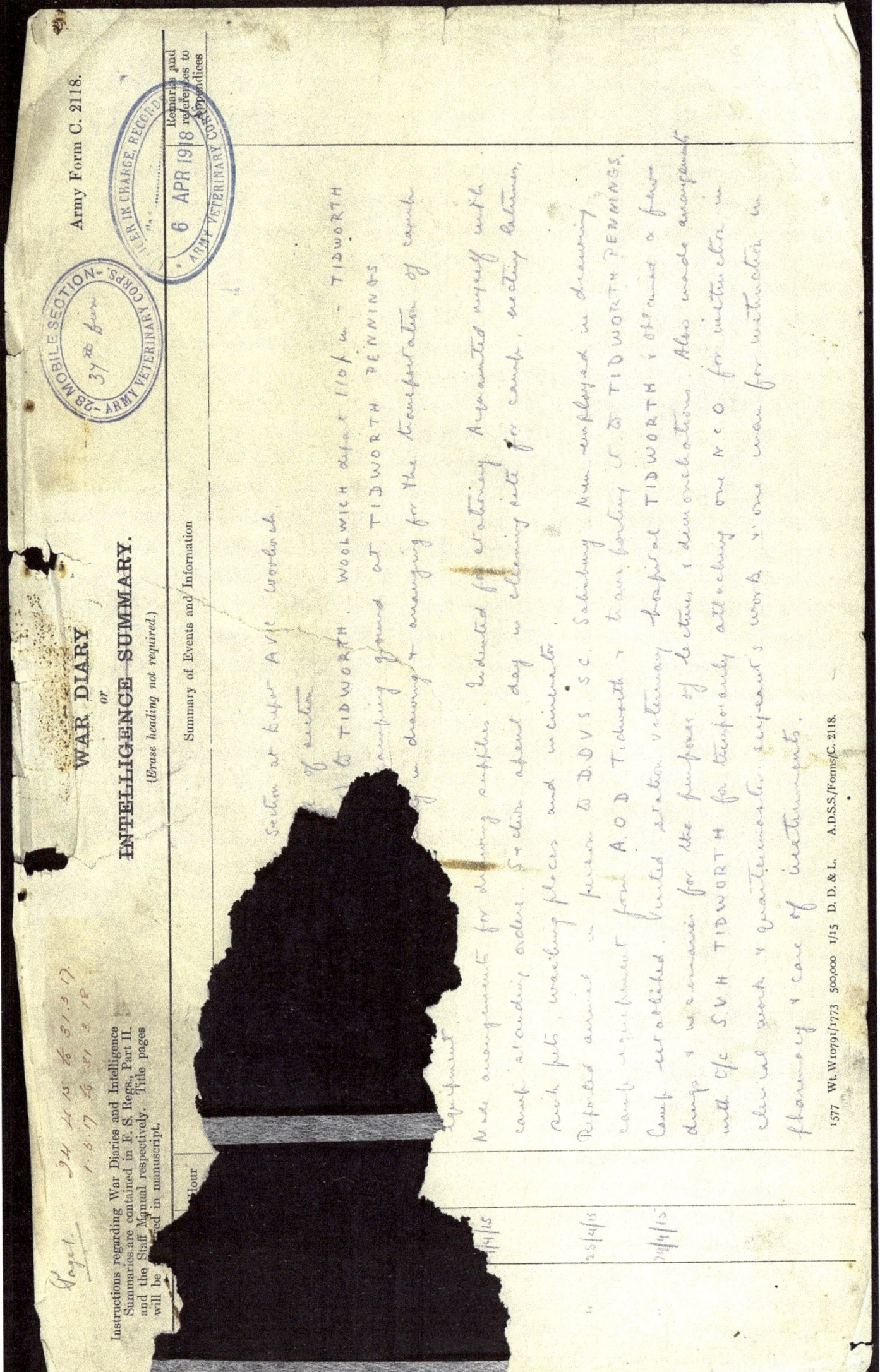

[illegible]	[illegible]	Hour	Summary of Events and Information	Remarks and references to Appendices
[illegible]	[illegible]		[illegible] Section at Depot AVC Woolwich	
			[illegible] of section	
			[illegible]) to TIDWORTH. WOOLWICH depart 1.10 p.m. - TIDWORTH	
			[illegible] camping ground at TIDWORTH PENNINGS	
			[illegible] in drawing + arranging for the transportation of camp equipment	
	[illegible]/4/15		Made arrangements for drawing supplies. Indented for stationery. Acquainted myself with camp standing orders. Section spent day in cleaning site for camp, erecting latrines, sink pits, washing places and incinerator.	
"	25/4/15		Reported arrival in person to D.D.V.S. S.C. Salisbury. Men employed in drawing camp equipment from A.O.D. Tidworth + transporting it to TIDWORTH PENNINGS.	
	26/4/15		Camp established. Visited station veterinary hospital TIDWORTH + obtained a few drugs + instruments for the purposes of lectures + demonstrations. Also made arrangements with O/c S.V.H. TIDWORTH for temporarily attaching one N.C.O. for instruction in clerical work + quartermaster-serjeant's work + one man for instruction in pharmacy + care of instruments.	

1577 Wt. W10791/1773 500,000 1/15 D. D. & L. A.D.S.S./Forms/C. 2118.

Page 2

Instructions regarding War Diaries and Intelligence Summaries are contained in F. S. Regs., Part II. and the Staff Manual respectively. Title pages will be prepared in manuscript.

WAR DIARY
or
~~INTELLIGENCE~~ SUMMARY.

(Erase heading not required.)

-28 MOBILE SECTION- ARMY VETERINARY CORPS.

Army Form C. 2118.

Place	Date	Hour	Summary of Events and Information	Remarks and references to Appendices
TIDWORTH	30/4/15		Issued standing orders for No 28 Mobile Veterinary Section. Drew up daily programme as follows:- Reveille 6 a.m. Drill 6.30 – 7.30. Clean camp 9 – 10. Lecture 10 – 1. Dinner 1 p.m. Drill 2.30. Lecture 3 – 4.30 Tea 5 p.m. Camp picquet mounts 6 p.m. Tattoo 9 p.m. Lights out 10 p.m.	
—			This day opened pay a/c with Paymaster S.C. & paid out section.	
			The lectures were based on the syllabus laid down in Appendix I Standing Orders Army Veterinary Corps – a few portions only being deleted. Subjects of lecture – morning – The points & conformation of the horse. Afternoon – handling & approaching horses.	
	1/5/15		Lecture morning – Fastening horses in stables & in the field. Afternoon – morning subject continued.	
	2/5/15		Lecture morning – Grooming & exercising. Afternoon Watering & feeding	
	3/5/15		Lecture morning & afternoon Bandaging.	
	4/5/15		Lecture morning – signs of health in the horse. Afternoon – signs of disease.	
	5/5/15		Lecture morning & afternoon } Pulse, temperature	
	6/5/15		Lecture morning & afternoon } & respirations.	
			Returned 6174 Pte J. K. Dunn to Depot AVC. Woolwich as medically unfit. Gave	

Page 3.

Instructions regarding War Diaries and Intelligence Summaries are contained in F. S. Regs., Part II. and the Staff Manual respectively. Title pages will be prepared in manuscript.

WAR DIARY
or
INTELLIGENCE SUMMARY.
(Erase heading not required.)

Army Form C. 2118.

Place	Date	Hour	Summary of Events and Information	Remarks and references to Appendices
TIDWORTH			instruction in putting down picketing gear & making horse lines. 6447 Pte W. Simpson arrived from Woolwich	
	7/5/15		Opened field veterinary hospital. One case admitted. Demonstrations morning & afternoon - methods of administering medicines	
	8/5/15		5 cases admitted. Demonstration on administering medicines continued	
	9/5/15		The arrival of sick horses necessitated alterations in the daily routine. Hence regular drill was stopped & the men grouped into dressers & sick line orderlies. It is intended to interchange these weekly so that each man may have the opportunity of dressing wounds & the administration of medicines	
	10/5/15		4 Cases admitted	
	11/5/15		8 Cases admitted (1 Died).	
	12/5/15		4 Cases admitted.	
	13/5/15		3 Cases admitted.	
	14/5/15		4 Cases admitted.	
	15/5/15		1 Case admitted. Total under treatment 29.	

A A Pryer
Commanding

Instructions regarding War Diaries and Intelligence Summaries are contained in F. S. Regs., Part II. and the Staff Manual respectively. Title pages will be prepared in manuscript.

WAR DIARY
or
INTELLIGENCE SUMMARY.
(Erase heading not required.)

Army Form C. 2118.

Place	Date	Hour	Summary of Events and Information	DAILY RETURN OF HORSES UNDER TREATMENT: ADMITTED	CURED	DESTROYED	DIED	TRANSFERRED	TOTAL REMAINING	Remarks and references to Appendices
Tidworth Pennings	May 16th		Particulars during this time to be filled in by Lieut Pryer	5					38	
	17th			8					40	
	18th			–					40	
	19th			6					46	
	20th		Lieut Pryer AVC removed to Tidworth Hospital on instructions of Med Officer in Attd							
			Lieut F.C Gillard AVC takes over Command of Section (Authority ADVS 37th Division	3					49	(A)
	21st		Mobilization Vety equipment recd for Units 37 Division							
				1	10	1 (B)			39	(A) Died of Pneumonia
	22nd		Ten Remounts for Section Staff arrive. Strength of Section Horses now 18							
				8		1 (B)			40	(B) Destroyed Poll Evil Case
			Strength of Section: NCOs 4, men 20; Horses: Officers chargers 8, Staff Horses 10 — week ending 29/5/15							

Instructions regarding War Diaries and Intelligence Summaries are contained in F. S. Regs., Part II. and the Staff Manual respectively. Title pages will be prepared in manuscript.

WAR DIARY
or
INTELLIGENCE SUMMARY.
(Erase heading not required.)

Army Form C. 2118.

-28 MOBILE SECTION- ARMY VETERINARY CORPS.

Place	Date	Hour	Summary of Events and Information	DAILY RETURN OF HORSES UNDER TREATMENT: ADMITTED	CURED	DIED	DESTROYED	TRANSFERRED	TOTAL REMAINING	Remarks and references to Appendices
Tidworth Pennings	May 23rd		ADVS visits Section Camp etc	3	4				39	
	24th		Shoeing Smith Brown of the Section detailed to attend of Lectures on Shoeing at Farriers Class under Mr Hayden Lectures on Shoeing to Wilts County Council	2					41	
	25th		The Ncos and men of the Section were inspected by Medical Officer re fitness for Service overseas and all reported fit	5					46	
	26th			2	2			2 (a)	44	(a) To SVH Bulford
	27th		ADVS visits & inspects Camp	1					45	
	28th		ADVS visits Section Camp							
	29th		ADVS visits Section Camp	1	1				45	
			Strength of Section: Ncos 4, men 26; Horses: Officer's Chargers 2, Staff Horses 10	2	5				42	

week ending 22/5/15

Instructions regarding War Diaries and Intelligence Summaries are contained in F. S. Regs., Part II. and the Staff Manual respectively. Title pages will be prepared in manuscript.

WAR DIARY
or
INTELLIGENCE SUMMARY.
(Erase heading not required.)

Army Form C. 2118.

Place	Date	Hour	Summary of Events and Information	Daily Return of Horses under Treatment: Admitted	Cured	Died	@ Destroyed	Transferred	Total Rem^g	Remarks and references to Appendices
Tidworth Pennings	May 30th		Lance Corp^l Wilson A.V.C reported himself for Duty in Error Detained pending inquiry (authority ADVS)	3	2		1		42	Destroyed when in @ extreme form Purpura - Septicaemia
	31st		ADVS visits Section Camp	2	3				41	
	June 1st		Lecture by O.C to N^cos & men of Section in Points of the Horse ADVS visits Section Camp	1					42	
	2nd		1 N^co and 4 men inoculated with A.T Lecture by O.C to N^cos & men of Section (Stable Duties etc)	2					44	
	3rd		Lecture by OC to men of the Section ADVS visits Section Camp	1	2			(B) 4	39	To SVH Bulford
	4th		1 N^co and 3 men inoculated with A.T	8					47	
	5th		Lecture by O C to men of the Section A.D.V.S visits Section Camp etc	2					49	

Strength of Section N^cos 4, men 20 } week ending 5/6/15
" " Horse O'Keeper 2
" Staff 10

1577 Wt. W10791/1773 500,000 1/15 D. D. & L. A.D.S.S./Forms/C. 2118.

Instructions regarding War Diaries and Intelligence Summaries are contained in F. S. Regs., Part II. and the Staff Manual respectively. Title pages will be prepared in manuscript.

WAR DIARY
or
INTELLIGENCE SUMMARY.
(Erase heading not required.)

-28 MOBILE SECTION- ARMY VETERINARY CORPS.

Army Form C. 2118.

Place	Date	Hour	Summary of Events and Information	DAILY RETURN OF HORSES UNDER TREATMENT: ADMTD	CURED	DIED	DESTROYED	TRANSFD	TOTAL REMG	Remarks and references to Appendices
Tidworth Pennings	June 6th		Lance Corpl. Wilson transferred to Bulford for Duty (Authority ADVS (letter) 20/3/15. Lecture by O C to men of Section. ADVS visit Section Camp	7	3	1	(a) 2	(b) 2	50	(a) Died for Strangles (b) To SVH Bulford
	7th		No 616 Lance Corpl. (a/Cpl.) John Barnes A.V.C. reverted to private at his own request. 1 NCO & 6 men inoculated with AT. Lecture to men of Section by O C	-	2				48	
	8th		Lecture by O C to men of Section. ADVS visits Section Camp							
	9th		4 men inoculated with AT Rifles 20 Revolvers & Bandoliers 20 drawn from Ordnance Stores Tidworth Lecture to NCOs & men of Section Bandaging etc	3	5				46	
	10th		Drew majority of Mobilization equipment from Ordnance Stores Tidworth. Lecture by O.C to men of Section	1				1 (c)	46	(c) To SVH Bulford
	11th		Vety Major Pallin RHS Inspected Camp and Examined the men of the							
	11		section in regard to their duties and on the subject of Horsemastership etc	1					47	
	11th		No 183 Corpl. A Harris AVC brought before O C on charge of Neglect of Duty was found guilty and was reprimanded 1 NCO & 3 men inoculated with A.T							

Instructions regarding War Diaries and Intelligence Summaries are contained in F. S. Regs., Part II. and the Staff Manual respectively. Title pages will be prepared in manuscript.

WAR DIARY
or
INTELLIGENCE SUMMARY.
(Erase heading not required.)

Army Form C. 2118.

Place	Date	Hour	Summary of Events and Information	DAILY RETURN OF HORSES UNDER TREATMENT: ADMITTED	CURED	DIED	DESTROYED	TRANSFERRED	TOTAL REMNG	Remarks and references to Appendices
Tidworth Pennings	June 13th		Daily Riding Drill for men of Section Commenced Lecture by OC to NCOs & men of the Section	5					52	
			Strength of Section NCOs 4, men 20 } week ending 12/6/15 " Horses OC 2 " Staff 10							

Instructions regarding War Diaries and Intelligence Summaries are contained in F. S. Regs., Part II. and the Staff Manual respectively. Title pages will be prepared in manuscript.

WAR DIARY
or
~~INTELLIGENCE SUMMARY.~~

(Erase heading not required.)

Army Form C. 2118.

Place	Date	Hour	Summary of Events and Information	In the Section	Admitted since	Cured	Destroyed	Transferred	Died	Remaining	Remarks and references to Appendices
TIDWORTH	2/7/15		1289 Pte W. WHEELER awarded 96 hours detention at Perham Down by O.C. for absence without leave.								
	3/7/15		A.D.V.S. visited camp and examined men on weeks lectures. Heavy showers. Received drugs from WOOLWICH which were urgently required.	79	4				1	83	

A A Pryer Lt
O/C 28 Mobile Vety Section.

Instructions regarding War Diaries and Intelligence Summaries are contained in F. S. Regs., Part II. and the Staff Manual respectively. Title pages will be prepared in manuscript.

WAR DIARY
or
INTELLIGENCE SUMMARY.
(Erase heading not required.)

Army Form C. 2118.

Place	Date	Hour	Summary of Events and Information	In last Return	Admitted	Destroyed	Died	Transferred	Cured	Remaining	Remarks and references to Appendices
TIDWORTH	4/7/15		Lecture on foods & watering	83	1	-	-	-	1		83
	5/7/15		Lecture on foodstuffs and their preparation. A D V S visits camp.	83	1	-	-	-	1		83
	6/7/15		62?? W. WHEELER relieved from detention barracks Perham Down. Lecture on feeding & watering completed	83	1	-	-	-	3		79
	7/7/15		A D V S visits camp. Two post mortems made & lecture on elementary anatomy of horse's alimentary tract.	79	1	2	-	1	11		66
	8/7/15		Lecture & demonstration on elementary anatomy of the fore limb. Conducting party to Bulford	66				8	3		55
	9/7/15		A D V S visits camp. Lecture & demonstration on administration of medicine and enemata. Drugs arrived from WOOLWICH	55	5	-	-	-	-		60
	10/7/15		A D V S visits camp and examines the section on the lectures of the week. The weather has been inclement during the week and thereby thrown back the progress of the training. It also delays the washing & dressing of severe cases of mange.	60	4	-	-	-	-		64

A A Pryce Lt AVC
OC 28th Mobile Vety Section

1577 Wt. W10791/1773 500,000 1/15 D. D. & L. A.D.S.S./Forms/C. 2118.

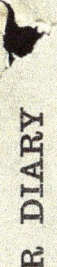

Instructions regarding War Diaries and Intelligence Summaries are contained in F. S. Regs., Part II. and the Staff Manual respectively. Title pages will be prepared in manuscript.

WAR DIARY
or
INTELLIGENCE SUMMARY.
(Erase heading not required.)

28 MOBILE SECTION — ARMY VETERINARY CORPS.

Army Form C. 2118.

Place	Date	Hour	Summary of Events and Information	Remained [illegible]	Admitted	Died	Destroyed	Transferred	Issued	Remaining	Remarks and references to Appendices
TIDWORTH	11/7/17		Held [illegible] inspection. Lecture on [illegible] [illegible]	64	7	-	-	-	-	71	
	12/7/17		A D V S held an inspection at 10 30 a m. Dress Field Service Marching order. Limbers packed	71	3	-	-	-	-	74	
	13/7/17		Operations during morning. Lecture on Bandaging and [illegible] [illegible]. Conducting party to Bulford	74	4	-	-	1	9	68	
	14/7/17		A D V S visited camp. Lecture on forage rations	68	4	-	-	3	-	69	
	15/7/17		Conducting party to Bulford. Lecture on [illegible] of health and disease. Received intimation that a horse sent to BULFORD on [illegible] had [illegible] [illegible] symptoms of [illegible]	69	5	-	-	-	8	66	
	16/7/17		A D V S visited camp. Lecture on elementary anatomy of the horse's foot. Heavy rain delayed work.	66	3	-	-	-	5	64	
	17/7/17		Further rain. A D V S visited [illegible] and [illegible] [illegible] on the [illegible] work. [illegible] [illegible] of [illegible] from horse [illegible] of [illegible] [illegible] [illegible]	64	4	-	-	-		68	

[illegible signature]

1577 Wt. W10791/1773 500,000 1/15 D. D. & L. A.D.S.S./Forms/C. 2118.

Instructions regarding War Diaries and Intelligence Summaries are contained in F. S. Regs., Part II. and the Staff Manual respectively. Title pages will be prepared in manuscript.

WAR DIARY
or
INTELLIGENCE SUMMARY.
(Erase heading not required.)

-28 MOBILE SECTION- ARMY VETERINARY CORPS.

Army Form C. 2118.

Place	Date	Hour	Summary of Events and Information	In last Return	Admitted Sick	Died	Destroyed	Transferred	Cured	Remaining	Remarks and references to Appendices
TIDWORTH	18-7-15		Heavy rain necessitating changing of lines.	68	-					68	
	19-7-15		A D V S. visited camp.	68	5					73	
	20-7-15		Heavy rain.	73	6			8	10	61	
	21-7-15		A D V S visited camp.	61	2					63	
	22-7-15		1st Sgt absent on 24 hours leave. 1st Sgt [illegible] i/c of unit	63	15					74	
	23-7-15		A D V S visited camp with a view to selecting horses fit for service and discharge to units & those unfit & to be transferred to [illegible]. At midnight telephone message received from A D V S stating that as a case of epizootic lymphangitis had been verified in 33rd Reserve Park all admissions & discharges from this Mobile Section were to cease until further orders.	74	1			1	30	30	
	24-7-15		This mobile section should have been cleared of sick this day under A D V S letter 235/15 dated 17/7/15 but owing to telephone message received at midnight no evacuation could take place. Instructions laid down in telephone	50			1			49	

Instructions regarding War Diaries and Intelligence Summaries are contained in F. S. Regs., Part II. and the Staff Manual respectively. Title pages will be prepared in manuscript.

WAR DIARY
or
INTELLIGENCE SUMMARY.
(Erase heading not required.)

-28 MOBILE SECTION- ARMY VETERINARY CORPS.

Army Form C. 2118.

Place	Date	Hour	Summary of Events and Information	Remarks and references to Appendices
TIDWORTH	24/7/15		Fatigue party to Ordnance Stores Tidworth. [illegible] complied with Heavy & un[illegible] hospital work. Owing to the large number of patients received & discharged during the week & the fact that a number of men were on leave time has been too fully occupied to permit of lectures being given during the past week 6732 Pte H. Thompson returned to Depot AVC Woolwich this day under escort as incompetable [illegible]. 10571 Pte R. WORTHY arrived to take his place 6259 Pte W. Wheeler forfeits 2 days pay for absence without leave 6022 Pte T GILBERT forfeits 2 days pay & awarded 7 days C B for absence without leave A A Payne Lt AVC O.C. 28th Mobile Vety Section	

1577 Wt. W10791/1773 500,000 1/15 D. D. & L. A.D.S.S./Forms/C. 2118.

Instructions regarding War Diaries and Intelligence Summaries are contained in F. S. Regs., Part II. and the Staff Manual respectively. Title pages will be prepared in manuscript.

WAR DIARY
or
INTELLIGENCE SUMMARY.
(Erase heading not required.)

Army Form C. 2118.

-28 MOBILE SECTION- ARMY VETERINARY CORPS.

Place	Date	Hour	Summary of Events and Information	Remaining	Admitted Sick	Died	Destroyed	Transferred	Cured	Remaining	Remarks and references to Appendices
TIDWORTH	25-7-15		Checked mobilization equipment. Drew ordnance stores to complete A. F. G 1098 - 89.	79	15	-	-	-	1	93	
	26-7-15		Received orders for embarkation for service overseas.	93	3	-	-	-	-	96	
	27-7-15.		Dispatched 9 horses by rail to Convalescent Horse Depot TAUNTON. Commenced evacuation of unfit to BULFORD	96	-	-	-	48	18	30	
	28-7-15.		Returned camp equipment with exception of tents and blankets to ordnance store. Closed camp equipment account and forwarded ledger to local auditor	30	32	-	-	36	-	26	
	29-7-15		Paid N.C.O's + men. Closed pay account and returned all documents + vouchers concerned to regimental paymaster	26	2		-	3	-	25	
	30-7-15		Visited every camp of the division collecting abandoned horses, - 7 horses and 2 mules collected + sent to BULFORD. Returned all documents to Officer i/c Records A.V.C.	25	14	-	-	39	-	Nil	
	31-7-15		Parade 10 a.m. Inspection of rifles, saddlery + kit. Parade for station prior to entraining 11.30 a.m.								

A A Pryer
Lt. A.V.C.
O.C. 28 Mobile Vety Section

T2134. Wt. W708—776. 500000. 4/15. Sir J. C. & S.

Army Form C. 2118.

Instructions regarding War Diaries and Intelligence Summaries are contained in F. S. Regs., Part II. and the Staff Manual respectively. Title pages will be prepared in manuscript.

WAR DIARY

or

~~INTELLIGENCE SUMMARY.~~

(Erase heading not required.)

-28 MOBILE SECTION- ARMY VETERINARY CORPS.

ASSISTANT DIRECTOR OF VETERINARY SERVICES 37th DIVISION No. C/18/15 Date 1.10.15

Place	Date	Hour	Summary of Events and Information	Remarks and references to Appendices
TIDWORTH	31.7.15	11 a.m.	Parade for service overseas. Marched to TIDWORTH station and entrain.	
		1.20 p.m.	TIDWORTH depart	
		3.40 p.m.	Arrive SOUTHAMPTON DOCKS and embarked on S.S. ANGLO-CANADIAN.	
		5 p.m.	Sailed from SOUTHAMPTON.	AAP
HAVRE	1.8.15	3.15 a.m.	Arrived M. PIERRE JANELLE reported for duty as interpreter.	
		NOON.	Completed disembarkation and marched to No 5 Rest Camp	
	2.8.15	7.30 a.m.	Parade to march to station for entraining.	
		11.55 a.m.	Train left HAVRE.	
		5 p.m.	Halt at MONTROLIER BUCHY	
		10.20 p.m.	Halt at ABBEVILLE.	AAP
TILQUES	3.8.15	6.30 a.m.	Arrived at AUDRIUCQ and detrained. Marched to billets at TILQUES. 2 horses admitted.	AAP
RENESCURE	4.8.15		Marched from TILQUES to billets at RENESCURE. arriving at 8.30 p.m. one horse collected from TOURNEHEM	AAP
CAESTRE	5.8.15		Marched from RENESCURE 3 p.m. to billets at CAESTRE arriving at 6.30 p.m.	AAP
	6.8.15		D.D.V.S. 2nd Army inspected the unit. 1 horse admitted.	AAP
FLÊTRE	7.8.15		Marched from RENESCURE 9.30 a.m. arriving in billets at FLÊTRE 12 noon. 11 horses admitted.	

T2134. Wt. W708—776. 500000. 4/15. Sir J. C. & S.

Instructions regarding War Diaries and Intelligence Summaries are contained in F. S. Regs., Part II. and the Staff Manual respectively. Title pages will be prepared in manuscript.

WAR DIARY
or
~~INTELLIGENCE SUMMARY.~~
(Erase heading not required.)

Army Form C. 2118.

Place	Date	Hour	Summary of Events and Information	Remarks and references to Appendices
FLÊTRE	8.8.15		With ~~[illegible]~~ collecting party to HONDEGHEM and LYNDE. 3 mules and 1 horse collected.	
"	9.8.15		Two horses admitted. Weather good. Nothing to report	
"	10.8.15		One horse admitted.	
"	11.8.15		Four horses admitted. Obtained money from Field Cashier and paid N.C.O.'s and men.	
"	12.8.15		Collecting party to EECKE, HONDEGHEM and SERCUS. Two horses collected. Nine horses	
"			admitted altogether.	
"	13.8.15		Two horses admitted.	
"	14.8.15		With A.D.V.S. to STEENVORDE to see horse with a view to collecting it.	
"	15.8.15		12 horses admitted. Nine horses and 4 mules evacuated by rail to No 10 Veterinary Hospital	
"	16.8.15		Sharp fall of rain.	
"	17.8.15		3 horses admitted. Rifle and respirator inspection.	
"	18.8.15		1 horse admitted.	
"	19.8.15		11 horses and 1 mule evacuated. 4 cases admitted.	
"	20.8.15		4 cases admitted.	
"	21.8.15		1 case admitted	
"	22.8.15		Church of England service at 9 30 a.m. 7 cases admitted.	

T2134. Wt. W708—776. 500000. 4/15. Sir J. C. & S.

Instructions regarding War Diaries and Intelligence Summaries are contained in F. S. Regs., Part II. and the Staff Manual respectively. Title pages will be prepared in manuscript.

WAR DIARY
or
~~INTELLIGENCE SUMMARY.~~
(Erase heading not required.)

Army Form C. 2118.

Place	Date	Hour	Summary of Events and Information	Remarks and references to Appendices
FLÊTRE	23.8.15		14 horses admitted. D.D.V.S 2nd Army inspected sick lines.	
"	24.8.15		16 horses and 1 mule evacuated. Smoke helmets for horses arrived. Preliminary instructions to move received.	A A Pryer. Lt
"	25.8.15		Lt A.A. PRYER fell sick and was removed to No. 12 Casualty Clearing Station. Lieut W. HUSTON from 124th Bde R.F.A. takes command of section. 2 horses admitted.	
"	26.8.15		21 horses evacuated. 5 admitted 2 of which were collected from CAESTRE.	
"	27.8.15		Marched out of billets at 3.30 a.m. and proceeded to CASSEL. Entrained at station and departed 9.50. Arrived MONDECOURT at 5 p.m. and marched to billets at AUTHIEUL arriving at 8 p.m.	
AUTHIEUL	28.8.15		The division has now left the 2nd Army and is incorporated in the 7th Corps, 3rd Army engaged in operations on the border between the departments of PAS de CALAIS and SOMME. Captain J. R. C. JONES. A.V.C. (T.F.) takes over command of the section from Lt HUSTON.	
"	29.8.15		A.D.V.S visits section. Heavy rain.	W Huston Lt.
"	30.8.15		A.D.V.S. visits section. One horse admitted.	
"	31.8.15		No admissions. Ordinary routine duties.	
"	1.9.15		No admissions.	
"	2.9.15		8 horses admitted.	

Instructions regarding War Diaries and Intelligence Summaries are contained in F. S. Regs., Part II. and the Staff Manual respectively. Title pages will be prepared in manuscript.

WAR DIARY
or
~~INTELLIGENCE~~ SUMMARY.
(Erase heading not required.)

-28 MOBILE SECTION- ARMY VETERINARY CORPS.

Army Form C. 2118.

Place	Date	Hour	Summary of Events and Information	Remarks and references to Appendices
AUTHIEUL	3.9.15		2 horses admitted. Weather bad. Men in open in bivouacs.	
"	4.9.15		Nothing to report.	
"	5.9.15		Section marched into new billets at MONDECOURT. Accomodation for horses and men is very good indeed. 2 horses admitted	
MONDECOURT	6.9.15		1 horse admitted. Much work done in arranging hospital. Prepared outhouse for use as a pharmacy. Disinfected & whitewashed garage as billet for men.	
"	7.9.15		2 horses admitted. A great deal of work done in cleaning and putting billet in order	
	8.9.15		Arranged for rifle and respirator inspection daily in accordance with Divisional Orders.	
	9.9.15		Three men reported as verminous. Outbreak attributed to a recent issue of blankets. Bath erected and measures taken as per medical officers recommendations. 2 horses admitted	
	10.9.15		Arranged for hire of float for use as an ambulance – this being very urgently required 3 cases admitted	
	11.9.15		Made preliminary investigations into the question of surface drainage of the courtyard of the billet & the erection of shelters for horses should we remain during the winter.	

I L C Jones
Capt. A V C

T2134. Wt. W708–776. 500000. 4/15. Sir J. C. & S.

Instructions regarding War Diaries and Intelligence Summaries are contained in F. S. Regs., Part II. and the Staff Manual respectively. Title pages will be prepared in manuscript.

WAR DIARY
or
~~INTELLIGENCE~~ SUMMARY.
(Erase heading not required.)

28 MOBILE SECTION - ARMY VETERINARY CORPS.

Army Form C. 2118.

Place	Date	Hour	Summary of Events and Information	Remarks and references to Appendices
MONDECOURT	12.9.15		Was able to obtain material for erection of shelters. Commenced to cart same and dump it close at hand. This work together with that of drainage will entail heavy work for some weeks to come. 7 horses admitted.	
"	13.9.15		Collecting party with float to AMPLIER. The question of a float is a very pressing one. At present this one (the only one in the district) has to be fetched some distance the owner making his own conditions. These entail its return each evening and it is only available when he does not require it himself. It has to be horsed by the supply waggon horses giving them too much additional work after their journey to the refilling point. Moreover the time of refilling is constantly changing and if near midday renders long journeys very difficult to arrange for. 11 horses admitted.	
"	14.9.15		Nothing to report.	
"	15.9.15		5 horses admitted. A.D.V.S. visited sick lines.	
"	16.9.15		8 horses evacuated.	
"	17.9.15		Nothing to report.	
"	18.9.15		2 horses admitted.	
"	19.9.15		Nothing to report.	

H.C. Jones
Capt. A.V.C.

T2134. Wt. W708–776. 500000. 4/15. Sir J. C. & S.

Instructions regarding War Diaries and Intelligence Summaries are contained in F. S. Regs., Part II. and the Staff Manual respectively. Title pages will be prepared in manuscript.

WAR DIARY
or
~~INTELLIGENCE SUMMARY.~~
(Erase heading not required.)

-28 MOBILE SECTION- ARMY VETERINARY CORPS.

Army Form C. 2118.

Place	Date	Hour	Summary of Events and Information	Remarks and references to Appendices
MONDECOURT	20.9.15		A.D.V.S. visits sick lines. Men reported free of vermin.	H C Jones Capt. A.V.C.
"	21.9.15		3 horses admitted. Lt. A.A PRYER rejoined from hospital and resumes command of the unit from Capt. JONES.	
"	22.9.15		1 horse admitted. A.D.V.S. visits section and selects cases for evacuation.	
"	23.9.15		1 horse admitted. 12 horses evacuated. Very heavy rain & lightning.	
"	24.9.15		3 horses admitted. Paid section.	
"	25.9.15		D.D.V.S. 3rd Army inspected section. Collecting party with float to GAUDIEMPRÉ.	
"	26.9.15		Mackintosh capes and further blankets arrived and were issued to the men. 1 Horse admitted. Heavy rain entailing shifting of horse lines.	
"	27.9.15		To POMMIER and LA BÉZAQUE to inspect horses for collection.	
"	28.9.15		4 Horses admitted. Outbreak of suspected glanders in Amm. Col. 125 Bde. R.F.A necessitated the application of the mallein test to the 3 animals from that unit under treatment in the field hospital. All reactions negative.	
"	29.9.15		3 Horses admitted. To railhead with 12 horses for evacuation – the float making 2 journies.	
"	30.9.15		German aeroplanes dropped bombs on the village at noon. No damage of military importance done. Men working on the construction of stables for winter quarters. 1 Horse admitted.	

A A Pryer. Lt. AVC.
O.C. 28 Mobile Vety Section 1.10.15

T2134. Wt. W708–776. 500000. 4/15. Sir J. C. & S.

37th Division

121/7595.

28th Mob: Vet: Sect.
Vol 2

Oct 15

Nil
Cu.

Instructions regarding War Diaries and Intelligence Summaries are contained in F. S. Regs., Part II. and the Staff Manual respectively. Title pages will be prepared in manuscript.

WAR DIARY
or
INTELLIGENCE SUMMARY.
(Erase heading not required.)

Army Form C. 2118.

-28 MOBILE SECTION- ARMY VETERINARY CORPS.

Place	Date	Hour	Summary of Events and Information	Remarks and references to Appendices
MONDICOURT.	1.10.15		4 Horses admitted. Work on stables continued	A.A.P.
"	2.10.15		Suit stable for 8 horses completed. 2 Horses admitted.	A.A.P.
"	3.10.15		2 Horses admitted	A.A.P.
"	4.10.15		4 Horses admitted. 4783 Pte. SCOTT A. transferred to No 46 Mobile Section vide Corps Orders No 34	A.A.P.
"	5.10.15		2 Horses admitted. 11 Horses evacuated	A.A.P.
"	6.10.15		8 Horses admitted.	A.A.P.
"	7.10.15		3 Horses admitted.	A.A.P.
"	8.10.15		6 Horses admitted. 8220 Actg. L/Cpl KEELY J and 8647 Actg L/Cpl. JENKINSON. W.H sent to No. 10 Veterinary Hospital in accordance with instructions from D.V.S.	A.A.P.
"	9.10.15		5 Horses admitted	A.A.P.
"	10.10.15		16 Horses admitted.	A.A.P.
"	11.10.15		10 Horses admitted.	A.A.P.
"	12.10.15		46 Horses evacuated. 17 Horses admitted.	A.A.P.
"	13.10.15		2 Horses admitted. S.E. 6185 Pte LUTHER. R.T. awarded 28 days Field Punishment No 1 for drunkeness by Commandant ABBEVILLE Escort sent to dispatch same	A.A.P.
"	14.10.15		3 Horses admitted	A.A.P.

T2151. Wt. W708—776. 500000. 4/15. Sir J. C. & S.

Instructions regarding War Diaries and Intelligence Summaries are contained in F. S. Regs., Part II. and the Staff Manual respectively. Title pages will be prepared in manuscript.

WAR DIARY
or
~~INTELLIGENCE~~ SUMMARY.
(Erase heading not required.)

Army Form C. 2118.

Place	Date	Hour	Summary of Events and Information	Remarks and references to Appendices
MONDICOURT	15.10.15		6 Horses admitted.	A.A.P.
"	16.10.15		28 Horses admitted. For the past week efforts have been taxed, the section is 5 below strength owing to men sick and an unusual number of horses are being admitted. Nearly all these are cases of debility evacuated from the Divisional Artillery by orders of A.D.V.S. 37th Div.	A.A.P.
"	17.10.15		5 Horses admitted.	A.A.P.
"	18.10.15		3 Horses admitted.	
"	19.10.15		3 Horses admitted. 51 Horses evacuated.	A.A.P.
"	20.10.15		4 Horses admitted.	A.A.P.
"	21.10.15		4 Horses admitted. 6208 Pte. BEATTIE. D. invalided to England	A.A.P.
"	22.10.15		11 Horses admitted.	A.A.P.
"	23.10.15		8 Horses admitted. 23 Horses evacuated	A.A.P.
"	24.10.15		5 Horses admitted.	A.A.P.
"	25.10.15		15 Horses admitted.	A.A.P.
"	26.10.15		2 Horses admitted. 29 Horses evacuated.	A.A.P.
"	27.10.15		3 Horses admitted. Heavy rain. All transport engaged in carting timber, material for building stables	A.A.P.

Instructions regarding War Diaries and Intelligence Summaries are contained in F. S. Regs., Part II. and the Staff Manual respectively. Title pages will be prepared in manuscript.

6/22/16
1.11.15

WAR DIARY
or
INTELLIGENCE SUMMARY.
(Erase heading not required.)

28 MOBILE SECTION ARMY VETERINARY CORPS.

Army Form C. 2118.

Place	Date	Hour	Summary of Events and Information	Remarks and references to Appendices
MONDICOURT	28.10.15		8 Horses admitted Heavy rain. Work on stables continued daily.	AAP
"	29.10.15		1 Horse admitted. Automatic horse clipper arrived which is of great assistance. It would seem in the light of recent experience that the authorisation of the following articles for a mobile veterinary section are needed viz lamps singeing, a blow lamp (this has now been obtained after difficulty as there was no authority for its issue. A field forge would be of the greatest possible assistance. If any query should be raised with regard to the difficulty of carrying the same with the existing transport it may be pointed out that under the present arrangement for the carriage of smoke helmets for horses by Mobile Veterinary Sections each section is immobile. The cubic space required by 750 smoke helmets requires a G. S. waggon to transport them. As the existing G. S. waggon is a supply waggon & is part of the Divisional Train & marches with the supply section of that unit it is not available to carry these helmets. Moreover even if it were there would not be sufficient space for them when the waggon is carrying the two days rations which have to be taken on the line of march. In event of a rapid move it is difficult to say how these could be carried. The issue of one bicycle for purposes of inter communication is also required	AAP
"	30.10.15		6 Horses admitted.	AAP
"	31.10.15		2 Horses admitted	AAP

A A Payne Lt AVC.
O.C. 28 Mobile Veterinary Section.

T2134. Wt. W708—776. 500000. 4/15. Sir J. C. & S.

37th Division

28th Inf: Vet: Sect.
Vol: 3

~~H.Q. 37th Division~~

~~A.D.V.S.~~

~~Vol. 4~~

121/7693

Nov. 15.
Dec. 15.

Nil
Am.

Instructions regarding War Diaries and Intelligence Summaries are contained in F. S. Regs., Part II. and the Staff Manual respectively. Title pages will be prepared in manuscript.

WAR DIARY
or
INTELLIGENCE SUMMARY.
(*Erase heading not required.*)

Army Form C. 2118.

Place	Date	Hour	Summary of Events and Information	Remarks and references to Appendices
MONDICOURT	1 11 15		6 Horses admitted.	AAP
"	2 11 15		17 Horses evacuated sick. At present the mornings are spent in general stable duties, dressing etc. but in the afternoons all available labour is devoted to the completion of stables for the winter.	AAP
"	3 11 15		2 Horses admitted	AAP
"	4 11 15		6 Horses admitted.	AAP
"	5 11 15		2 Horses admitted 6176 Pte C. CRABTREE awarded 14 days Field Punishment No 1 for when on active service – drunkeness	AAP
"	6 11 15		(1 Horse admitted) It has now been possible to obtain a small supply of sawdust for use as litter and it is noticeable that it apparently possesses a remarkable curative effect on wounds of the feet and lower extremities. The sawdust used is obtained from sawing deal i.e. various varieties of fir & one would imagine that the healing properties are due to the terpene derivatives contained therein.	AAP
"	7 11 15		13 Horses admitted.	
"	8 11 15		6 Horses admitted SE 6259 Pte W. WHEELER invalided to England on this date.	AAP
"	9 11 15		2 Horses admitted. 24 horses evacuated	AAP

T2134. Wt. W708–776. 500000. 4/15. Sir J. C. & S.

Instructions regarding War Diaries and Intelligence Summaries are contained in F. S. Regs., Part II. and the Staff Manual respectively. Title pages will be prepared in manuscript.

WAR DIARY
or
INTELLIGENCE SUMMARY.
(Erase heading not required.)

Army Form C. 2118.

Place	Date	Hour	Summary of Events and Information	Remarks and references to Appendices
MONDICOURT	10 11 15		4 Horses admitted	AAP
"	11-11-15		8 Horses admitted.	AAP
"	12 11 15		2 Horses admitted.	AAP
"	13 11 15		5 Horses admitted	AAP
"	14 11 15		7 Horses admitted	AAP
"	15 11 15		8 Horses admitted	AAP
"	16 11 15		Heavy spell of snow during early morning 25 Horses evacuated 1 Horse admitted	AAP.
"	17 11 15		2 Horses admitted S E 6022 Pte GILBERT T invalided to England on this date	
			This unit is now 3 men understrength and has been wanting men to complete for over a month. Needless to say, in so small a formation this is a very serious handicap and it would be of great assistance if reinforcements could be more promptly dispatched. A man cannot be struck off the strength until notification has been received from the Officer i/c Base Records by which time he may have already been sick in this country for any period up to six weeks. Hence it appears that a period of nearly three months is required in some cases to replace a casualty. Notes to this effect have been and are being made	

T2134. Wt. W708–776. 500000. 4/15. Sir J. C. & S.

Instructions regarding War Diaries and Intelligence Summaries are contained in F. S. Regs., Part II. and the Staff Manual respectively. Title pages will be prepared in manuscript.

WAR DIARY
or
INTELLIGENCE SUMMARY.
(Erase heading not required.)

-28 MOBILE SECTION- ARMY VETERINARY CORPS.

Army Form C. 2118.

Place	Date	Hour	Summary of Events and Information	Remarks and references to Appendices
MONDICOURT	17 11 15		weekly on A F B 213 but without result.	A.A.P.
"	18 11 15		Nothing to report	A.A.P.
"	19 11 15		3 Horses admitted – 2 collected from GAUDIEMPRÉ. Weather extremely cold with sharp frosts	A.A.P.
"	20 11 15		18 Horses admitted – 2 collected from SOUASTRE	A.A.P.
"	21 11 15		10 Horses admitted	A.A.P.
"	22 11 15		6 Horses admitted.	A.A.P.
"	23 11 15		3 Horses admitted 24 Horses evacuated	A.A.P.
"	24 11 15		6 Horses admitted. Owing to the increasing darkness in the morning reveille is postponed from 5.30 – 6.0	A.A.P.
"	25 11 15		4 Horses admitted. The five following men received this day from No 9 Veterinary Hospital	
			DIEPPE. Authority A V C Base Records T/135 of 19/11/15.	
			S E 454 Pte RICE J.	
			S E 2284 " RIX E	
			S.E 2354 " THORN W	
			S E 2585 " TUCKER F.F	
			S.E. 2566 " PHIPPS D.A	A.A.P.
"	26 11 15		4 Horses admitted. The following five men dispatched this day to No 9 Veterinary	

T2134. Wt. W708–776. 500000. 4/15. Sir J. C. & S.

Instructions regarding War Diaries and Intelligence Summaries are contained in F. S. Regs., Part II. and the Staff Manual respectively. Title pages will be prepared in manuscript.

WAR DIARY
or
INTELLIGENCE SUMMARY.
(Erase heading not required.)

Army Form C. 2118.

-28 MOBILE SECTION- ARMY VETERINARY CORPS.

Place	Date	Hour	Summary of Events and Information	Remarks and references to Appendices
MONDICOURT	26 11 15		Hospital DIEPPE in exchange for the five privates received yesterday.	
			SE 6103 Pte VINYARD A.	
			SE 6176 " CRABTREE C	
			SE 6188 " SMITH A R.	
			S.E. 6190 " SPENCER F.	
			SE 6285 " MORRIS B E.	AAP
"	27 11 15		2 Horses admitted. 15 horses evacuated.	AAP
"	28 11 15		5 Horses admitted. Intense frost & cold.	AAP.
"	29 11 15		8 Horses admitted. Heavy rain throughout the day.	AAP.
"	30 11 15		4 Horses admitted. 14 Horses Evacuated 1 Case collected in float from HENU.	AAP
			<u>Resumé of Work Done</u>	
			During the past month much labour has been expended in erecting winter quarters and improving existing conditions for both horses and men. Material has been carted on the sections own limited transport and stabling for 65 horses has been erected. Existing buildings have been improved and if necessary provide accomodation for a further 25 horses & when completed will be increased to 50.	

T2134. Wt. W708—776. 500000. 4/15. Sir J. C. & S.

Instructions regarding War Diaries and Intelligence Summaries are contained in F. S. Regs., Part II. and the Staff Manual respectively. Title pages will be prepared in manuscript.

WAR DIARY
or
INTELLIGENCE SUMMARY.
(Erase heading not required.)

Army Form C. 2118.

28 MOBILE SECTION – ARMY VETERINARY CORPS.

Place	Date	Hour	Summary of Events and Information	Remarks and references to Appendices
MONDICOURT	30.11.15		The whole of this work has been done by the men of the section (which has been from 3 to 5 men under strength during the entire period). No assistance whatsoever has been received from the R.E. or other unit expected to assist in construction and transport. The men have worked well and appear interested and the amount of crime is very moderate considering the difficulties one is confronted with in transforming civilians of mature age into soldiers in so short a time.	
			It may be of interest to quote statistics showing the purely veterinary work done during the period Aug 4th – Nov 30th – slightly less than four months.	
			531 cases have been admitted to the section which were disposed of as follows.	
			Died 4	
			Destroyed 12	
			Cured 88	
			Evacuated 393	
			Remaining 34	
			Total 531	
			I am of the opinion that the percentage returned to duty as cured would be larger if the demands made on my time as an executive veterinary officer were not so heavy thus enabling me to give more personal attention to cases in the hospital.	AAP
			A A Pryer Lt AVC.	
			OC 28 Mobile Veterinary Section.	

T2134. Wt. W708—776. 500000. 4/15. Sir J. C. & S.

Instructions regarding War Diaries and Intelligence Summaries are contained in F. S. Regs., Part II. and the Staff Manual respectively. Title pages will be prepared in manuscript.

WAR DIARY
or
INTELLIGENCE SUMMARY.
(Erase heading not required.)

-28 MOBILE SECTION- ARMY VETERINARY CORPS. 37th Divn

Army Form C. 2118.

Place	Date	Hour	Summary of Events and Information	Remarks and references to Appendices
MONDICOURT	1.12.15		10 horses admitted Continued stable construction.	A.A.P.
	2.12.15		6 Horses admitted	A.A.P.
	3.12.15		7 Horses admitted.	A.A.P.
	4.12.15		13 Horses admitted	A.A.P.
	5.12.15		10 Horses admitted. 28 Animals conducted to railhead and evacuated	A.A.P.
	6.12.15		2 Animals admitted. The section was this day inspected by the G.O.C 37th Divn who offered his congratulations & expressed himself as much pleased with the work done.	A.A.P.
	7.12.15		3 Horses admitted. By this date all plans for winter building for adding to the comfort of men and horses are complete with the exception of the men's bathroom. Much time & labour is however taken up every day in keeping the buildings in repair & in carting cinders & sawdust for preserving horse standings.	A.A.P.
	8.12.15		3 Horses admitted	A.A.P.
	9.12.15		3 Horses admitted Weather stormy & heavy fall of rain	A.A.P.
	10.12.15		2 Horses admitted	A.A.P.
	11.12.15		3 Horses admitted.	A.A.P.

Instructions regarding War Diaries and Intelligence Summaries are contained in F. S. Regs., Part II. and the Staff Manual respectively. Title pages will be prepared in manuscript.

WAR DIARY
or
INTELLIGENCE SUMMARY.
(Erase heading not required.)

Army Form C. 2118.

Place	Date	Hour	Summary of Events and Information	Remarks and references to Appendices
MONDICOURT	12.12.15		5 Horses admitted.	A.A.P.
	13.12.15		4 Horses admitted.	A.A.P.
	14.12.15		13 Horses admitted. 22 Animals conducted to railhead & evacuated.	A.A.P.
	15.12.15		3 Horses admitted.	
	16.12.15		3 Horses admitted.	
	17.12.15		In accordance with instructions received from D.V.S per A.D.V.S. 37th Divn. all animals in the section - 72 in number - were this day subjected to the intra dermal palpebral mallein test.	A.A.P.
	18.12.15		1 Horse admitted.	A.A.P.
	19.12.15		2 Horses admitted. No reactors whatsoever to the mallein test.	A.A.P.
	20.12.15		30 Animals admitted.	A.A.P.
	21.12.15		4 Animals admitted. Lt PRYER goes sick and is to be transferred to 50th Field Ambulance in the morning. Capt. J.L.C. JONES. AVC. arrives from 37th Divnl. Train A.S.C. on being posted to temporary command of the section.	
			A A Pryer Lt AVC OC 28th Mobile ~~Veterinary~~ Section	A.A.P.

T2134. Wt. W708–776. 500000. 4/15. Sir J. C. & S.

Instructions regarding War Diaries and Intelligence Summaries are contained in F. S. Regs., Part II. and the Staff Manual respectively. Title pages will be prepared in manuscript.

WAR DIARY
or
INTELLIGENCE SUMMARY.
(Erase heading not required.)

-28 MOBILE SECTION- ARMY VETERINARY CORPS.

Army Form C. 2118.

Place	Date	Hour	Summary of Events and Information	Remarks and references to Appendices
	1915.			
MONDICOURT.	Dec 22nd.		Took over the Section from Lieut Pryer A.V.C. on Sick Leave.	JLCJ
"	" 23rd		Carried on usual work of the Section.	JLCJ
	" 24		Section work as usual. Visited 37th Divl A.C. & Examined Sick Animals	JLCJ
	" 25		Usual Section work	JLCJ
	" 26		Section work. Visited D.A.C. Sick Animals	JLCJ
	" 27		Carried on usual Section work. Visited D.A.C.	JLCJ
	" 28		Section work & Sundry repairs to Horse Shelters carried out	JLCJ
	" 29		Section work. Visited D.A.C.	JLCJ
	" 30		Section work. Visited D.A.C.	JLCJ.
	" 31.		Usual Section work.	JLCJ.
			The Section during the month has been regularly visited & inspected by the	JLCJ.
			A.D.V.S. 91 Horses have been Tested with Mallein. 198 Horses admitted	JLCJ.
			32 Horses Discharged & 155 Evacuated.	JLCJ.

T2134. Wt. W708–776. 500000. 4/15. Sir J. C. & S.

28th Inf: Vet: Sect:
Vol: 4

37

Instructions regarding War Diaries and Intelligence Summaries are contained in F. S. Regs., Part II. and the Staff Manual respectively. Title pages will be prepared in manuscript.

WAR DIARY
or
INTELLIGENCE SUMMARY.
(Erase heading not required.)

Army Form C. 2118.

Place	Date	Hour	Summary of Events and Information	Remarks and references to Appendices
MONDICOURT	Jan 1st		Ordinary work of the Section carried on. 1 Case discharged "Cured." 10 Admitted.	J.L.C.J.
"	" 2nd		Ordinary Section work 27 Animals admitted.	J.L.C.J.
"	" 3rd		Ordinary Section work carried on – 2 animals discharged Cured. 140 Animals of	J.L.C.J.
"	–		the D.A.C. Tested with Mallein by the Palpebral Method. 12 Admission	J.L.C.J.
"	4th		Section work as usual. 6 Animals admitted – 49 Animals discharged to Base	J.L.C.J.
"			Visited & Examined Tested animals of the D.A.C.	J.L.C.J.
"	5th		Usual Section work – 15 admissions	J.L.C.J.
"	6th		11 animals were admitted to the Section – 1 Discharged Cured. Visited D.A.C. no reactions	J.L.C.J.
"	7th		4 admission – The usual work of the Section carried on.	J.L.C.J.
"	8th		2 admission – Section work as usual – 3 Animals discharged Cured & 68 sent	J.L.C.J.
"	"		to the Base, "Evacuated" –	
"	9th		Section work as usual – 13 animals admitted – 8 discharged Cured	J.L.C.J.
"	10th		Usual Section work – 3 animals admitted. 3 discharged Cured.	J.L.C.J.
"	11th		Section work as usual – practiced men with Smoke Helmets.	J.L.C.T.
"			53 Animals admitted.	J.L.C.T.
	12th		Section work as usual	J.L.C.T.

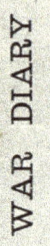

Instructions regarding War Diaries and Intelligence Summaries are contained in F. S. Regs., Part II. and the Staff Manual respectively. Title pages will be prepared in manuscript.

WAR DIARY
or
INTELLIGENCE SUMMARY.
(Erase heading not required.)

Army Form C. 2118.

Place	Date	Hour	Summary of Events and Information	Remarks and references to Appendices
MONDECOURT	13-1-16		Section work as usual. Visited D.A.C. Tested 102 mules with mallein. 13 animals discharged	JLCJ
"	14-1-16		Usual Section work - Visited D.A.C. & examined Tested mules.	JLCJ
"	15-1-16		Section work - Visited Tested mules D.A.C. ~~Evacuated~~ admitted 45 animals to Section	JLCJ
"	16-1-16		Section work 3 animals admitted to Section	JLCJ
-	17-1-16		Usual Section work. 4 animals admitted	JLCJ
-	18-1-16		Section work. 11. animals admitted	JLCJ
-	19-1-16		Section work. 12 animals admitted	JLCJ
-	20-1-16		Section work. 63 animals Evacuated & 5 admitted - 5 discharged to units	JLCJ
-	21/1/16		Section work 14 animals admitted	JLCJ
-	22-1-16		Section work - 6 animals admitted. Visited D.A.C	JLCJ
-	23-1-16		Section work - 6 animals admitted	JLCJ
-	24-1-16		Section work 3 animals admitted - Visited D.A.C.	JLCJ
-	25-1-16		Section work 3 animals admitted	JLCJ
-	26-1-16		Section work 4 animals admitted Visited D.A.C	JLCJ
-	27-1-16		Section work 4 animals admitted - 28 Evacuated - 7 Discharged	JLCJ
-	28-1-16		Section work 4 animals admitted Visited D.A.C.	JLCJ.

Instructions regarding War Diaries and Intelligence Summaries are contained in F. S. Regs., Part II. and the Staff Manual respectively. Title pages will be prepared in manuscript.

WAR DIARY
or
INTELLIGENCE SUMMARY.
(Erase heading not required.)

Army Form C. 2118.

Place	Date	Hour	Summary of Events and Information	Remarks and references to Appendices
MONDECOURT.	29/1/16		Section work _ 2 Horses admitted to Section	JRCJ
–	30/1/16		Section work. 2 animals admitted	JRCJ
–	31/1/16		Section work.	JRCJ
			During the month the section has been regularly visited & inspected by the	JRCJ.
			A.D.V.S. There has been a large number of admission & Evacuation due to	JRCJ.
			an outbreak of Contagious Skin Disease about the latter part of December last	JRCJ.
			Admissions 309 animals	JRCJ.
			Evacuated 269. " "	JRCJ.
			Discharged 28. " "	JRCJ.
			Animals Tested with Mallein 594.	JRCJ.

T2134. Wt. W708–776. 500000. 4/15. Sir J. C. & S.

21/28 ? Mil: Vet: Secr:

Vol: 5

Instructions regarding War Diaries and Intelligence Summaries are contained in F. S. Regs., Part II. and the Staff Manual respectively. Title pages will be prepared in manuscript.

WAR DIARY
or
INTELLIGENCE SUMMARY.
(Erase heading not required.)

Army Form C. 2118.

Place	Date	Hour	Summary of Events and Information	Remarks and references to Appendices
MONDECOURT	1/2/16		Section work as usual	JLCJ
"	2/2/16		Section work as usual	JLCJ
"	3/2/16		Section moved out of MONDECOURT to GRINCOURT.	JLCJ
GRINCOURT.	4/2/16		Section work carried on as usual - Commenced to build Shelters for animals of the Section	JLCJ
"	5/2/16		Section work & carried on building operations	JLCJ
"	6/2/16		Section work, building & admitting lame animals from units 40 animals admitted	JLCJ
"	7/2/16		Usual Section work. 38 Animals Evacuated Completed Shelters for 17 animals	JLCJ
"	8/2/16		Section work as usual	JLCJ
"	9/2/16		Section work as usual	JLCJ
"	10/2/16		Section work as usual - Busy Erecting Shelters - 50. animals admitted	JLCJ
"	11/2/16		Usual Section work 50 animals Evacuated	JLCJ
"	12/2/16		Usual Section work - Busy Erecting Shelters	JLCJ
"	13/2/16		Usual Section work - Busy getting Cinders & Sawdust for Shelter floors.	JLCJ
"	14/2/16		Usual Section work	JLCJ
"	15/2/16		Section work as usual Shelters erected for 29 Horses.	JLCJ

Instructions regarding War Diaries and Intelligence Summaries are contained in F. S. Regs., Part II. and the Staff Manual respectively. Title pages will be prepared in manuscript.

WAR DIARY
or
INTELLIGENCE SUMMARY.
(Erase heading not required.)

Army Form C. 2118.

28 MOBILE SECTION – ARMY VETERINARY CORPS. 37th Divn

Place	Date	Hour	Summary of Events and Information	Remarks and references to Appendices
GRINCOURT	16/2/16		Usual Section work	ILCJ
	17/2/16		Section work	ILCJ
	18/2/16		Usual Section work – Advanced Collecting Station posted at LARBRET.	ILCJ
	19/2/16		Usual Section work – Disinfecting & Cleansing standings for 15 Horses at Advanced Post.	ILCJ
	20/2/16		Usual Section work. 57 Animals admitted – 7 animals floated in Horse Ambulance	ILCJ.
	21/2/16		Section work as usual.	
	22/2/16		Capt. A A PRYER rejoined unit from England and resumes command of section. Heavy fall of snow 1 horse admitted 49 Horses & Mules evacuated.	A.A.P.
	23/2/16		Continued frost & snow greatly impeding work. Capt. T. L. C. JONES leaves section on being posted to 37th Divl. Train. A.S.C.	A.A.P.
	24/2/16		4 Horses admitted. Fatigue party engaged in transporting building material from PAS to section billets.	A.A.P.
	25/2/16		1 Horse admitted. More building material recovered. Continued snow & frost.	A.A.P.
	26/2/16		Searched Divisional Area for more suitable billets without success. More snow.	A.A.P.
	27/2/16		Commenced erection of more stables.	A.A.P.
	28/2/16		30 animals admitted. A.D.V.S visited section	A.A.P.
	29/2/16		64 Horses & mules evacuated	A.A.P.

A A Pryer. Capt. A.V.C.
O.C. 28th Mobile Vety. Section

T2134. Wt. W708–776. 500000. 4/15. Sir J. C. & S.

28 M V See

vol 6

Instructions regarding War Diaries and Intelligence Summaries are contained in F. S. Regs., Part II. and the Staff Manual respectively. Title pages will be prepared in manuscript.

WAR DIARY
or
INTELLIGENCE SUMMARY.
(Erase heading not required.)

-28 MOBILE SECTION- ARMY VETERINARY CORPS. 37th Divn.

Army Form C. 2118.

Place	Date	Hour	Summary of Events and Information	Remarks and references to Appendices
GRINCOURT	1.3.16		Visited Advanced Collecting Station. Building operations proceeded with	AAP.
	2.3.16		Two horses admitted. Section engaged in constructing stables & improving billets.	AAP
	3.3.16		Visited Advanced Collecting Station & A.D.V.S. 9 horses admitted. Paid NCO's & men.	AAP.
	4.3.16		Heavy fall of snow greatly hindering work. 1 Horse admitted.	AAP.
	5.3.16		Continued snow fall. Usual section work.	AAP.
	6.3.16		29 Horses & 5 Mules admitted.	AAP.
	7.3.16		33 Horses & 6 Mules evacuated. 1 Horse destroyed. Visited Advanced Collecting Station	AAP.
	8.3.16		Building of stables proceeded with. Sawdust & timber carted on section transport.	AAP.
	9.3.16		A.D.V.S. visited section. Pharmacy built	
	10.3.16		Congratulatory message received from D.V.S. saying the work of the section reflected the greatest credit on all concerned. This message read out to section on parade in accordance with instructions received from D.D.V.S. 3rd Army. Forwarded the names of S.E. 6724 Sergt. P. F FLOOD and S.E. 4936 Corpl. S.A.N. LAMBERT to 37th Divn as being especially worthy of reward. Visited A.D.V.S. and Advanced collecting station.	AAP.
	11.3.16		1 Horse & 1 Mule admitted. Collected mule from M. TRIPET LOMBERT at HUMBERCOURT	AAP

T2134. Wt. W708—776. 500000. 4/15. Sir J. C. & S.

Instructions regarding War Diaries and Intelligence Summaries are contained in F. S. Regs., Part II. and the Staff Manual respectively. Title pages will be prepared in manuscript.

WAR DIARY
or
INTELLIGENCE SUMMARY.
(Erase heading not required.)

-28 MOBILE SECTION- 37th Divn ARMY VETERINARY CORPS.

Army Form C. 2118.

Place	Date	Hour	Summary of Events and Information	Remarks and references to Appendices
GRINCOURT	12.3.16		Section work as usual	A.A.P.
"	13.3.16		Section open for the reception of animals. 26 cases admitted 5 of which were	
"	[redacted]		collected in float.	A.A.P.
"	14.3.16		A D V S 4th Divn visited section with a view to placing No 4 Mobile Veterinary Section in the same billets on the 37th Division proceeding for rest into Army Reserve which I am warned is expected to occur shortly. 31 Horses & Mules Evacuated. 2 Horses admitted.	A.A.P.
"	15.3.16		Visited No 4 Mobile Veterinary Section at GROUCHES in company with A. D. V. S. 37th Divn. with a view to taking over their billets on proceeding into rest. Am much disappointed at the exchange whereby both men & horses will be deprived of much comfort. 2 Horses admitted. Great improvement in weather.	A.A.P.
	16.3.16		Visited Advanced Collecting Station in morning. Took 1 N C O & 10 men to represent the section at the funeral of Lieut. J. M. WHITE. A.V.C. 37th Divn. at HENU in the afternoon. 2 Horses admitted.	
	17.3.16		To conference at A. D. V. S.'s office in afternoon & visited advanced Collecting Station Paid out the section. 17 Horses admitted	A.A.P.
	18.3.16		Evacuated 29 horses & mules. weather dull. 6 Horses admitted	A.A.P.

Instructions regarding War Diaries and Intelligence Summaries are contained in F. S. Regs., Part II. and the Staff Manual respectively. Title pages will be prepared in manuscript.

WAR DIARY
or
INTELLIGENCE SUMMARY.
(Erase heading not required.)

-28 MOBILE SECTION- 37th Div. ARMY VETERINARY CORPS.

Army Form C. 2118.

Place	Date	Hour	Summary of Events and Information	Remarks and references to Appendices
GRINCOURT	19.3.16		Closed down Advanced Collecting Station at ~~[illegible]~~ LARBRET & sent personnel from there	
"			with portion of baggage to GROUCHES as advanced party for purposes of taking	
"			over from No 4 M.V.S. 5 horses admitted	AAP.
GROUCHES	20.3.16		7 horses admitted. Marched from GRINCOURT at 2 p.m. into billets in rest	
"			at GROUCHES (arr. 4 p.m.). Visited by A.D.V.S. 5 horses unable to travel left at	
"			GRINCOURT with No 4 M.V.S.	AAP.
"	21.3.16		Day spent in erecting latrines & cleaning billets & stables. Weather dull. Am	
"			appointed Town Major of GROUCHES from this date	A.A.P.
"	22.3.16		2 Horses admitted. Commenced erection of new cook house & preparation of barrack	
			room for men. One man joined from No 1 Convalescent Horse Depot	AAP.
"	23.3.16		Men occupied in erecting cook house. Whitewashing buildings for mess room and office.	
			Visited 50th Field Ambulance & Q.O. Yorkshire Dragoons to which units I am executive V.O.	A.A.P.
"	24.3.16		Commenced erection of new stables. Visited A.D.V.S.	A.A.P.
"	25.3.16		Party to BOQUEMAISON station at 9 a.m. to collect headcollars from remounts arriving	
			A.D.V.S. visited section. Office completed and occupied this day	A.A.P.
"	26.3.16		1 Horse died. Fatigue party dug grave for same. Party working on surface drainage of yard & billets	

T2134. Wt. W708—776. 500000. 4/15. Sir J. C. & S.

Instructions regarding War Diaries and Intelligence Summaries are contained in F. S. Regs., Part II. and the Staff Manual respectively. Title pages will be prepared in manuscript.

WAR DIARY
or
INTELLIGENCE SUMMARY.
(Erase heading not required.)

Army Form C. 2118.

Place	Date	Hour	Summary of Events and Information	Remarks and references to Appendices
GROUCHES	27.3.16		Work continued on buildings. 7 Horses admitted.	A.A.P.
	28.3.16		14 Horses evacuated from BOQUEMAISON. Visited 50th Field Ambulance at HAUTE VISÉE.	A.A.P.
	29.3.16		Brick building & work of repairing vehicles, saddlery, & bringing up mobilization equipment to full establishment continued now that the Division is in rest. To BOQUEMAISON with a view to collecting a mule that had been left. Visited O.C. Yorkshire Dragoons at BEAUREPAIRE.	A.A.P.
	30.3.16		Ambulance to BEAUREPAIRE. Inspected 3rd Bridging Train R.E at MILLY and took over veterinary charge of them.	A.A.P.
	31.3.16		Ambulance to MILLY to collect horse with tetanus. Visited A.D.V.S. 37th Div at LUCHEUX.	A.A.P.

A.A. Pryer
Capt. A.V.C.
O.C. 28th Mobile Veterinary Section
37th Division

Instructions regarding War Diaries and Intelligence Summaries are contained in F. S. Regs., Part II. and the Staff Manual respectively. Title pages will be prepared in manuscript.

WAR DIARY
or
INTELLIGENCE SUMMARY.
(Erase heading not required.)

~~XXX~~VII

-28 MOBILE SECTION- ARMY VETERINARY CORPS. 37th Div

28 MVets

Army Form C. 2118.

Vol. 7

Place	Date	Hour	Summary of Events and Information	Remarks and references to Appendices
GROUCHES	1.4.16		Usual section work. Greatly improved weather conditions enabling horses to be stood in the open during the day. Inspected Q.O. Yorkshire Dragoons. Summoned to DOULLENS at night to attend case of colic. Fatigue party to MONDICOURT for sawdust.	A.A.P.
	2.4.16		Instructing men in further mounted drill, extending etc & also musketry exercises. A.D.V.S visited section. 4 Horses admitted. Two stables now completed. Much time occupied in claims, billets & other Town Major's duties.	A.A.P.
	3.4.16		Usual section work. A.D.V.S. visited section	A.A.P.
	4.4.16		8 Animals evacuated from BOQUEMAISON. Visited 50th Field Ambulance.	A.A.P.
	5.4.16		Usual section work.	A.A.P.
	6.4.16		To BOQUEMAISON to select site for railhead dressing station.	A.A.P.
	7.4.16		23 animals evacuated. 3 horses collected from LE SOUICH. To conference at A.D.V.S. Office	A.A.P.
	8.4.16		2 animals collected from DOULLENS. Visited Q.O. Yorkshire Dragoons	A.A.P.
	9.4.16		D.D.V.S. visited section.	A.A.P.
	10.4.16		1 Horse admitted. Stabling now complete. Heavy rain. A.D.V.S. visited section.	A.A.P.
	11.4.16		1 Horse admitted. 17 Animals evacuated	A.A.P.
	12.4.16		8 Horses admitted. Oven built & latrines improved. Visited 50th Field Ambulance & Yorkshire Dragoons	A.A.P.

T2134. Wt. W708–776. 500000. 4/15. Sir J. C. & S.

Instructions regarding War Diaries and Intelligence Summaries are contained in F. S. Regs., Part II. and the Staff Manual respectively. Title pages will be prepared in manuscript.

WAR DIARY
or
INTELLIGENCE SUMMARY.
(Erase heading not required.)

-28 MOBILE SECTION- 37th Div ARMY VETERINARY CORPS

Army Form C. 2118.

Place	Date	Hour	Summary of Events and Information	Remarks and references to Appendices
GROUCHES	13.4.16		Day spent in Town Majors duties viz settling claims, numbering billets & ascertaining exact water supply	AAP
"	14.4.16		Nothing to report. Usual section work. Visited A.D.V.S.' office in afternoon	AAP
"	15.4.16		17 horses admitted. 15 N.C.O's & men of the section fired musketry course on Divisional Range at LUCHEUX in afternoon. Considering that this was the first occasion on which many of the men had fired their rifles the shooting was decidedly good.	AAP
"	16.4.16		4 Horses admitted	
"	17.4.16		6 Horses admitted. Waggons cleaned. Fatigue party to fetch sawdust for bedding from MONDICOURT	AAP
"	18.4.16		35 animals evacuated from BOQUEMAISON. Visited 50th Field Ambulance	AAP
"	19.4.16		Day spent in Town Majors duties arranging billets for 123rd Bde R.F.A. who came to the village this day. 4 Horses admitted	AAP
"	20.4.16		Remainder of personnel of section fired musketry course at LUCHEUX. Visited Yorkshire Dragoons	AAP
"	21.4.16		7 Horses admitted. Visited A.D.V.S. office at LUCHEUX	AAP
"	22.4.16		7 Horses admitted. Usual section work	AAP
"	23.4.16		4 Horses admitted. 7 men received anti typhoid inoculation.	AAP
"	24.4.16		5 Horses admitted. A.D.V.S. visited section	AAP

T2134. Wt. W708—776. 500000. 4/15. Sir J. C. & S.

Instructions regarding War Diaries and Intelligence Summaries are contained in F. S. Regs., Part II. and the Staff Manual respectively. Title pages will be prepared in manuscript.

WAR DIARY
or
INTELLIGENCE SUMMARY.
(Erase heading not required.)

-28 MOBILE SECTION- 37th Divn ARMY VETERINARY CORPS

Army Form C. 2118.

Place	Date	Hour	Summary of Events and Information	Remarks and references to Appendices
GROUCHES	25.4.16		25 Animals evacuated from BOQUEMAISON. Visited 50th Field Ambulance. Owing to the fact that in addition to commanding the section, I am executive V.O. to 300 horses & Town Major I have this day appealed that I may be relieved of the last named appointment. The pressure of work entailed by all three renders it impossible for me to carry out any one of them thoroughly & to my satisfaction.	A.A.P.
"	26.4.16		35 Animals admitted. Mostly cases of debility from the Divisional Artillery	A.A.P.
"	27.4.16		30 Animals admitted. All work is now at very high pressure. 56 animals evacuated from BOQUEMAISON. 22 for which railway transport is not available are left on the hands of the section.	A.A.P.
"	28.4.16		7 Animals admitted. Visited A.D.V.S. office in afternoon.	A.A.P.
"	29.4.16		Section inspected by D.D.V.S. 3rd Army who expressed himself as satisfied with what he saw. Relieved of Town Major's appointment	A.A.P.
"	30.4.16		21 Animals admitted. Received orders at 3 p.m. to move on May 2nd into the billets previously occupied at GRINCOURT & LARBRET & now held by 4th Div. M.V.S. who are to take over my present billets. Commenced making arrangements with O.C. No 4 M.V.S. accordingly & prepared for large evacuation tomorrow morning. A.A. Pryer Capt. AVC O.C. 28th Mobile Vety Section	A.A.P.

T2134. Wt. W708–776. 500000. 4/15. Sir J. C. & S.

Instructions regarding War Diaries and Intelligence Summaries are contained in F. S. Regs., Part II. and the Staff Manual respectively. Title pages will be prepared in manuscript.

WAR DIARY
or
INTELLIGENCE SUMMARY.
(Erase heading not required.)

Army Form C. 2118.

Vol 8

XXXVII

Place	Date	Hour	Summary of Events and Information	Remarks and references to Appendices
GROUCHES	1.5.16		63 animals evacuated from BOQUEMAISON. Sent advance party with portion of equipment to GRINCOURT. The withdrawal of one of the G.S. limbered waggons previously held on the establishment of a Mobile Veterinary Section would appear to be a severe handicap. The ambulance is unsuitable in every way for the conveyance of stores & although it has greater capacity than a G.S. waggon the transport of the section is still too small. This can be shown by load tables for the mobilization equipment of the unit together with the question of forage & rations. The carriage of an extra days rations as is frequently ordered renders the section immobile. These circumstances are emphasised even more by moving at present with the additional equipment that accumulates with stationary warfare & which would have to be disposed of prior to an advance.	A.A.P.
"	2.5.16		Ordered to move to GRINCOURT countermanded at noon. Further instructions received to proceed to SAULTY & to share billets with 55th Divn Mobile Vety Section. As most of the move was now completed at GRINCOURT authority was received to stay there temporarily. Completed move to GRINCOURT at 4 p.m. & also detached 1 NCO. & 2 men to 4 [illegible] Advanced Collecting Station at LARBRET. Rode personally to 55th Divn Mobile Section in	

T2134. Wt. W708-776. 500000. 4/15. Sir J. C. & S.

Instructions regarding War Diaries and Intelligence Summaries are contained in F. S. Regs., Part II. and the Staff Manual respectively. Title pages will be prepared in manuscript.

WAR DIARY

or

~~INTELLIGENCE SUMMARY.~~

(Erase heading not required.)

28 MOBILE SECTION – ARMY VETERINARY CORPS – 37th Divn.

Army Form C. 2118.

Place	Date	Hour	Summary of Events and Information	Remarks and references to Appendices
GRINCOURT	2.5.16		evening & found it impossible to close up with that unit who have received no orders to move.	A.A.P.
"	3.5.16		Rode round new divisional area to search for more suitable billet than SAULTY where the supply of water causes anxiety & the billet is congested with other troops. Noted the appearance of an isolated farm SONCAMP (FRANCE Map Sheet 57C. O 35a.)	A.A.P.
"	4.5.16		Section work as usual. Receive information that 110th Inf Bde are to occupy a portion of the SAULTY billet which will reduce the accomodation even more.	A.A.P.
"	5.5.16		Instruction from A.D.V.S. 37th Divn. to be clear of GRINCOURT by noon tomorrow. Visit his office in afternoon & suggest the necessity & finding the necessary accomodation at SONCAMP which we visited in evening. Decide to occupy it subject to approval of G.O. & Q.M.G. 37th Divn.	A.A.P.
"	6.5.16		Approval granted by A.A.Q.M.G. March from GRINCOURT at 2.30 p.m. to SONCAMP. Leave 1 NCO. & 2 men with 10 sick horses at GRINCOURT to be at LARBRET station for evacuation ~~to~~ tomorrow at 3.30 p.m. Established camp at SONCAMP.	A.A.P.
"	7.5.16		Men cleaning new billets etc. 20 horses & mules evacuated. Heavy rain	A.A.P.

Instructions regarding War Diaries and Intelligence Summaries are contained in F. S. Regs., Part II. and the Staff Manual respectively. Title pages will be prepared in manuscript.

WAR DIARY
or
~~INTELLIGENCE SUMMARY.~~
(Erase heading not required.)

Army Form C. 2118.

Place	Date	Hour	Summary of Events and Information	Remarks and references to Appendices
SONCAMP	8 5 16		Morning - office - Afternoon to LARBRET Evening office. ADVS visited section.	A.A.P.
"	9.5.16		Morning - attending sick. A.D.V.S. granted 8 days leave to England so take over his duties.	
			Afternoon A.D.V.S.' office. Evening own office.	A.A.P.
"	10 5 16		Morning - attending sick. Afternoon to A.D.V.S. office + LARBRET Evening own office.	A.A.P.
"	11 5 16		Morning attending sick. Afternoon with collecting party to WARLINCOURT and SOUASTRE.	
			One horse + 1 mule collected. Thence to A.D.V.S. office + home	A.A.P.
"	12.5.16		Prepared for evacuation next day. Held weekly conference of V.O's at A.D.V.S office in afternoon.	
			Thence to Advanced Collecting Station at LARBRET. Evening office.	A.A.P.
"	13.5.16		Morning - office + sick lines. Afternoon to LARBRET. 40 horses and mules evacuated.	
			Barn converted into stabling this day affording cover for 30 animals. Evening to A.D.V.S. office	
			to prepare returns for the Division to send to D.D.V.S. 3rd Army.	A.A.P.
"	14.5.16		Morning - office. Afternoon sick lines. The inclemency of the weather greatly impedes work.	A.A.P.
"	15.5.16		Morning sick lines + office. Afternoon to Field Cashiers Office + Divnl Headquarters. Attended to	
			A.D.V.S. correspondence + visited Advanced Collecting Station on return journey. 1 man sent on leave.	A.A.P.
"	16.5.16		Morning sick lines + with collecting party to SOMBRIN. 2 horses collected. Afternoon to A.D.V.S.	
			office at BAVINCOURT. Men engaged in building oven, painting vehicles and taking	

Instructions regarding War Diaries and Intelligence Summaries are contained in F. S. Regs., Part II. and the Staff Manual respectively. Title pages will be prepared in manuscript.

WAR DIARY
or
~~INTELLIGENCE SUMMARY.~~
(Erase heading not required.)

28 MOBILE SECTION - ARMY VETERINARY CORPS
37th Divn.

Army Form C. 2118.

Place	Date	Hour	Summary of Events and Information	Remarks and references to Appendices
SONCAMP	16.5.16		cured horses back to units.	A.A.P.
"	17.5.16		Morning sick lines. Afternoon to A.D.V.S.' office at BAVINCOURT. Evening own office. Greatly improved weather conditions enabling horses to remain in the open.	A.A.P.
"	18.5.16		Morning office & sick lines. Afternoon paid N.C.O's & men & held saddlery inspection. Thence to Divl. H'dqrs. calling at LARBRET on return journey.	A.A.P.
"	17.5.16		Morning office & sick lines. Afternoon to BAVINCOURT to hand over A.D.V.S. work to Major PALLIN who returned from leave this day	A.A.P.
"	20.5.16		Morning office & sick lines preparing for evacuation. Afternoon to Advanced Collecting Station and railhead. 18 horses & mules evacuated from LARBRET.	A.A.P.
"	21.5.16		Morning sick lines. Afternoon office. A.D.V.S. visited section. Owing to the breaking up of D.F.A. Bde Ammunition Columns the following three sergeants A.V.C. who have become surplus were this day attached to me pending orders as to their disposal. S.E. 2362 Sgt. FOSSIT. E. S.E. 2653 Sgt. WATSON. G. S.E. 4403 Sgt. GOODMAN. E.	A.A.P.
"	22.5.16		Morning sick lines & office. Afternoon to units at WARLUZEL	A.A.P.
	23.5.16		Inspected D.F.A. Brigade Amm. Cols. Surplus N.C.O.'s posted	A.A.P.
	24.5.16		20 Horses & mules admitted. 23 cases evacuated. Heavy rain.	A.A.P.

T2134. Wt. W708—776. 500000. 4/15. Sir J. C. & S.

Instructions regarding War Diaries and Intelligence Summaries are contained in F. S. Regs., Part II. and the Staff Manual respectively. Title pages will be prepared in manuscript.

WAR DIARY
or
INTELLIGENCE SUMMARY.
(Erase heading not required.)

Army Form C. 2118.

-28 MOBILE SECTION- ARMY VETERINARY CORPS. 37th Divn.

Place	Date	Hour	Summary of Events and Information	Remarks and references to Appendices
SONCAMP	25.5.16		Morning inspected 147 A.T. Coy. R.E. Afternoon sick lines. Evening office	A.A.P.
"	26.5.16		Morning sick lines & to units at WARLULEL. Afternoon D.A.D.V.S. office at BAVINCOURT. Evening office.	A.A.P.
"	27.5.16		Morning office & visited by A.A. & Q.M.G. 37th Divn. Afternoon sick lines. Evening to 48th Field Amb. at COUTERELLE to arrange for medical attendance on the section. 1 Horse destroyed for tetanus. No rain but weather still dull. Afternoon held kit inspection.	A.A.P.
"	28.5.16		Morning office. A.D.V.S. visited section. Afternoon – sick lines.	A.A.P.
"	29.5.16		Morning sick lines. Afternoon to Advanced Collecting Station, railhead & D.A.D.O.S. office. Evening – office.	A.A.P.
"	30.5.16		Morning sick lines. Afternoon 29 horses & mules evacuated from LARBRET. Thence to Advanced Collecting Station. Evening office.	A.A.P.
"	31.5.16		Morning sick lines, office & to Field Cashier at BAVINCOURT. Afternoon & evening – office	A.A.P.

A.A. Pryer Capt. A.V.C.
O.C. 28th Mobile Veterinary Section
37th Division.

T2134. Wt. W708–776. 500000. 4/15. Sir J. C. & S.

Instructions regarding War Diaries and Intelligence Summaries are contained in F. S. Regs., Part II. and the Staff Manual respectively. Title pages will be prepared in manuscript.

WAR DIARY or ~~INTELLIGENCE SUMMARY.~~ XXXVII

(Erase heading not required.)

-28 MOBILE SECTION- ARMY VETERINARY CORPS. 37th Divn

Army Form C. 2118.

Vol 9

Place	Date	Hour	Summary of Events and Information	Remarks and references to Appendices
SONCAMP.	1.6.16		Called urgently to Divl Hdqrs at 9.30 a.m. Found that Major PALLIN. A.D.V.S. 37th Divn had gone sick & was being removed to 48th Field Ambulance. Took over his duties which occupied until 6 p.m. Evening did section sick lines & office. Paid out NCO's & men	A.A.P.
"	2.6.16		Morning sick lines & office. Afternoon to A.D.V.S. office. Held weekly conference of V.O's & prepared returns for D.D.V.S. 3rd Army.	A.A.P.
"	3.6.16		Morning sick lines, office & to 48th Field Amb to see Major PALLIN. Afternoon to Divl Headquarters.	A.A.P.
"	4.6.16		Heavy rain during the greater part of the day. Morning sick lines & office. A.D.V.S. duties in afternoon & evening. Prepared for evacuation next day & visited advanced collecting station.	A.A.P.
"	5.6.16		15 animals evacuated. Continuation of rainy weather. Men employed in carting manure from yard & vicinity of billet. A.D.V.S. duties in afternoon & evening. Inspected D/123 owing to occurrence of a case of suspected mange.	A.A.P.
"	6.6.16		Morning sick lines & office. Afternoon to Collecting Station & thence to do A.D.V.S.' duties. Prepared for evacuation next day. The VIIth Corps has ruled that M.V. Sections must comply to the orders generally in force with regard to leading horses viz. one man is not to be in charge of more than two horses at once & that the led horse must be provided with bit & rein. The latter portion of course cannot be complied with & there are no bits & reins authorised for such a	

T2134. Wt. W708–776. 500000. 4/15. Sir J. C. & S.

Instructions regarding War Diaries and Intelligence Summaries are contained in F. S. Regs., Part II. and the Staff Manual respectively. Title pages will be prepared in manuscript.

WAR DIARY
or
INTELLIGENCE SUMMARY.
(Erase heading not required.)

Army Form C. 2118.

Place	Date	Hour	Summary of Events and Information	Remarks and references to Appendices
SONCAMP	6.6.16		purpose. The restriction as to leading one horse only seriously interferes with the efficient working of a section & in event of a large & speedy evacuation would be likely to disorganise it. Appeal was made to D.D.V.S. 3rd Army without satisfaction. Hence it becomes necessary to evacuate very often & in small numbers.	A.A.P.
"	7.6.16		Two cases of mange & suspected mange evacuated. Morning sick lines & office. Afternoon A.D.V.S. duties.	A.A.P.
"	8.6.16		At present the number of admissions of sick animals is lower than it has ever been - probably owing to improved weather conditions & the abolition of R.F.A. Bde Amm. Columns who always had exceptionally large numbers of sick. Heavy rain.	A.A.P.
"	9.6.16		Morning sick lines & office & inspected 147 A.T. Coy. R.E. Afternoon to weekly conference of V.O's at BAVINCOURT & prepared weekly veterinary returns for D.D.V.S. 3rd Army.	A.A.P.
"	10.6.16		Morning sick lines & office & to visit Major PALLIN at 48th Field Ambulance. Railhead & vicinity of Advanced Collecting Station heavily shelled from 5 a.m. till 9 a.m. Many shells blind. In afternoon to Advanced Collecting Station & had to send SE. 4936 Corpl LAMBERT the NCO i/c there sick. Wired to Officer i/c AVC Base Records reporting 153 Sergt Harris A. as an absentee. This NCO was due to return from 8 days special leave to England to see his sick wife on 5/6/16 & has not reported.	

Instructions regarding War Diaries and Intelligence Summaries are contained in F. S. Regs., Part II. and the Staff Manual respectively. Title pages will be prepared in manuscript.

WAR DIARY
or
INTELLIGENCE SUMMARY.
(Erase heading not required.)

Army Form C. 2118.

28 MOBILE SECTION - ARMY VETERINARY CORPS. 37th Divn

Place	Date	Hour	Summary of Events and Information	Remarks and references to Appendices
SONCAMP	10.6.16		This with two NCO's short & two men sick makes matters extremely difficult. However I am fortunate in having the loan of the services of SE. Sergt. 4403 GOODMAN. E. attached C/123 R F A. It is rumoured that railhead is likely to move back to MONDICOURT or even DOULLENS in consequence of this mornings bombardment. The former would be as convenient for entraining sick as LARBRET with the exception of float cases. The latter would entail a great strain being 12 miles to railhead. In any case the Advanced Collecting Station will not be of much value & will probably have to be abandoned. In evening to BAVINCOURT & handed over A.D.V.S. duties to Major PALLIN who returned to duty at 6 p.m.	A.A.P.
"	11.6.16		Dispatched SE. 4403 Sergt. GOODMAN. E to take over temporary charge of the ADVANCED Collecting Station at LARBRET. Morning sick lines. Afternoon - office	A.A.P.
"	12.6.16		S. E. 869 A/Cpl. McALESTER. R. joined section on this date. Authority Officer i/c A.V.C Base Records 5/26/16 d/- 21.5.16. Morning sick lines & visited 147 A.T. Coy R.E. Afternoon inspected by A.D.V.S. 37th Divn. Evening office. Received instructions that DOULLENS is now railhead & accordingly prepare to close down Advanced Collecting Station.	A.A.P.
"	13.6.16		Received instructions from A.D.V.S. at 9 a.m. that LARBRET was again to be used as a railhead from 14th prox. & that Advanced Collecting Station was to be maintained. To LARBRET & BAVINCOURT in morning.	

T2134. Wt. W708—776. 500000. 4/15. Sir J. C. & S.

Instructions regarding War Diaries and Intelligence Summaries are contained in F. S. Regs., Part II. and the Staff Manual respectively. Title pages will be prepared in manuscript.

WAR DIARY
or
INTELLIGENCE SUMMARY.
(Erase heading not required.)

-28 MOBILE SECTION- ARMY VETERINARY CORPS. 37th Div.

Army Form C. 2118.

Place	Date	Hour	Summary of Events and Information	Remarks and references to Appendices
SONCAMP	13.6.16		Afternoon sick lines & office & prepared for evacuation next day.	A.A.P.
"	14.6.16		Morning sick lines & office. Afternoon to LARBRET. 20 animals evacuated (4 mange cases & 2 float cases). 183 Sergt. Harris returned from special leave to see sick wife which had been extended from 5/6/16 until 12/6/16 by Officer i/c A.V.C. Records Woolwich. Sergt Harris posted as NCO i/c Advanced Collecting Station. SE. 4403 Sergt Goodman E who has been temporarily attached to section since the Amm. Col. 123rd Bde. was disbanded was this day posted to C/123. During the past few days a form of influenza seems to have broken out amongst the men of this & other units. 1 NCO & 2 men are sick & others complain of feeling unwell.	A.A.P.
"	15.6.16		8 Horses admitted. Morning sick lines & office. Afternoon to Field Cashier's Office PAS for money. Paid NCO's & men of section. 4936 Corpl. LAMBERT discharged to duty from 49th Field Ambulance.	A.A.P.
"	16.6.16		Bathing parade to village baths COUTURELLE at 10 a.m. Morning sick lines & office. Then improving water supply. Afternoon to weekly conference at A.D.V.S. office. Received instructions to strike 183 Sergt. HARRIS. A. off the strength & to dispatch him to Depot A.V.C. WOOLWICH on his being posted to the home command owing to the serious illness of his wife. Authority D.V.S. 2/2326/16 d/- 11/6/16.	

T2134. Wt. W708–776. 500000. 4/15. Sir J. C. & S.

Instructions regarding War Diaries and Intelligence Summaries are contained in F. S. Regs., Part II. and the Staff Manual respectively. Title pages will be prepared in manuscript.

WAR DIARY
or
INTELLIGENCE SUMMARY.
(Erase heading not required.)

Army Form C. 2118.

Place	Date	Hour	Summary of Events and Information	Remarks and references to Appendices
SONCAMP	17.6.16		Sick lines & office in morning. 183 Sgt HARRIS A dispatched to WOOLWICH on posting to the Home Command. To LARBRET in evening to inspect 15 horses that had been admitted from 124th Bde R.F.A. Preparing for evacuation next day. Considerable improvement in weather conditions.	A.A.P.
"	18.6.16		S.E. 881 Sgt MOYES J. Joined from No 1 Veterinary Hospital in lieu of 183 Sgt Harris A - to England. Morning sick lines, office & preparing for evacuation. Afternoon to Advanced Collecting Station & railhead. 31 horses & mules evacuated. Fatigue party with limber to Ordnance. Evening - church service.	A.A.P.
"	19.6.16		Morning sick lines & office. Afternoon rode up to villages behind the first line with a view to prospecting the country in event of a forward movement & to consider the possibility of throwing out Advanced First Aid Posts. Thence to Advanced Collecting Station.	A.A.P.
"	20.6.16		Sick lines & office. Thence to LARBRET where 24 animals had been admitted. Prepared for evacuation at once at sent the convoy from railhead at 5 p.m. Thence to A.D.V.S. office	A.A.P.
"	[redacted]		S.E. 6724 Sgt. FLOOD posted in orders this day as mentioned in the C in C's dispatch dated 30th April 1916 for gallant & distinguished conduct in the field.	A.A.P.
"	21.6.16		Morning sick lines & office. Afternoon to LARBRET. Evening office.	A.A.P.
"	22.6.16		Morning sick lines & office. 40 animals admitted. Afternoon to LARBRET. Preparing for evacuation next day.	A.A.P.

Instructions regarding War Diaries and Intelligence Summaries are contained in F. S. Regs., Part II. and the Staff Manual respectively. Title pages will be prepared in manuscript.

WAR DIARY
or
~~INTELLIGENCE SUMMARY.~~
(Erase heading not required.)

-28 MOBILE SECTION- ARMY VETERINARY CORPS. 37th Divn

Army Form C. 2118.

Place	Date	Hour	Summary of Events and Information	Remarks and references to Appendices
SONCAMP	23.6.16		Morning preparing for evacuation. 56 horses & mules conducted to railhead & evacuated. To LARBRET & A.D.V.S.'s office.	A.A.P.
"	24.6.16		Morning sick lines & office. Afternoon to LARBRET & preparing for evacuation next day.	A.A.P.
"	25.6.16		LARBRET railhead & COUTURELLE attacked by hostile aircraft. No damage done to section. Morning to 48th Field Ambulance at 11 a.m. to see four horses which had been wounded. Thence to Advanced Collecting Station & railhead. 34 horses & mules evacuated. A.D.V.S at railhead. Evening to 147 A.T Coy R.E.	A.A.P.
"	26.6.16		Morning sick lines & offices. 2 animals admitted. Heavy bombardment along Divisional front & much rain	A.A.P.
"	27.6.16		Morning sick lines & office. several minor operations performed including extraction of projectile from gunshot wounds. Afternoon to Advanced Collecting Station. Fatigue party to MONDICOURT for sawdust	A.A.P.
"	28.6.16		Rifle & respirator inspection. Fatigue party to railhead to collect headcollars from in coming remounts. Saddlery inspection in afternoon. Preparing for evacuation next day. Very heavy rain.	A.A.P.
"	29.6.16		Fatigue party to MONDICOURT for sawdust. Morning sick lines & office & to Field Cashier's office at PAS Thence to Advanced Collecting Station & found ambulance had made two journeys during previous night to POMMIER & BAVINCOURT for wounded horses. 17 Horses & Mules evacuated making a total of 107 in seven days A heavy week	A.A.P.

Instructions regarding War Diaries and Intelligence Summaries are contained in F. S. Regs., Part II. and the Staff Manual respectively. Title pages will be prepared in manuscript.

WAR DIARY
or
INTELLIGENCE SUMMARY.
(Erase heading not required.)

Army Form C. 2118.

-28 MOBILE SECTION- ARMY VETERINARY CORPS. 37th Div

Place	Date	Hour	Summary of Events and Information	Remarks and references to Appendices
SONCAMP	30.6.16		Morning sick lines & office. Afternoon to A.D.V.S. office at BAVINCOURT for weekly conference of V.O's. Evening - office preparing end of the month returns	A.A.P.
			A.A.Pryer Capt. AVC Cmdg. 28th Mobile Veterinary Section 37th Division 3rd Army.	

T2134. Wt. W708-776. 500000. 4/15. Sir J. C. & S.

Army Form C. 2118.

Instructions regarding War Diaries and Intelligence Summaries are contained in F. S. Regs., Part II. and the Staff Manual respectively. Title pages will be prepared in manuscript.

WAR DIARY

~~or~~

~~INTELLIGENCE SUMMARY.~~

(Erase heading not required.)

-28 MOBILE SECTION- ARMY VETERINARY CORPS. 37th Divn.

Vol 10

Place	Date	Hour	Summary of Events and Information	Remarks and references to Appendices
SONCAMP	1.7.16		Morning sick lines & office. Afternoon to A.D.V.S.' office & Advanced Collecting Station. Evening to see lame horse at LUCHEUX as per instructions received from A.D.V.S. 37th Divn. Fatigue party to MONDICOURT for sawdust.	A.A.P.
"	2.7.16		Morning sick lines & office. Afternoon inspected 147(A.T.) Coy R.E. & then was called on by A.D.V.S. 37th Divn who verbally gave me the following information & orders:— Owing to the military situation resulting on the recent fighting the 37th Divn was being withdrawn from the line & for the moment was going into reserve in an area roughly enclosing the following villages — PAS, FAMENCHON, HALLOY, HUMBERCOURT, WARLINCOURT which are in 46th Divn Area. The unit under my command ~~is~~ to move into the old billet at GRINCOURT which is now being vacated by 1/1st North Midland M.V.S. The move to be completed by Tuesday morning 4th prox. Consequently communication was established with O.C. 1/1st North Midland M.V.S. who probably will come to SONCAMP. Preparing for evacuation next day and issued orders for the detachment at the Advanced Collecting Station at LARBRET to make ready to close down & march to SONCAMP at 5 pm. next day.	A.A.P.
"	3.7.16		Considerable difficulty encountered in obtaining trucks for the convoy to ABBEVILLE owing to the demand on them made by wounded men. Eventually secured 3 trucks and evacuated 23 animals from LARBRET. Handed over Advanced Collecting Station to 46th Divnl M.V.S.	

T2134. Wt. W708—776. 500000. 4/15. Sir J. C. & S.

Instructions regarding War Diaries and Intelligence Summaries are contained in F. S. Regs., Part II. and the Staff Manual respectively. Title pages will be prepared in manuscript.

WAR DIARY
or
~~INTELLIGENCE SUMMARY.~~
(Erase heading not required.)

Army Form C. 2118.

Place	Date	Hour	Summary of Events and Information	Remarks and references to Appendices
SONCAMP	3.7.16		at 5 pm. & my N.C.O. & detachment returned with their transport to SONCAMP. Personally I then proceeded to GRINCOURT to make final arrangements as to taking over. Returned to SONCAMP at 9 p.m. & issued operation orders for next day	A.A.P.
GRINCOURT	4.7.16		Loading transport & cleaning billets from reveille onwards until breakfast. Marched out at 10.35 am arriving at GRINCOURT 11.50 am. Heavy rain. To PAS in afternoon to report completion of relief to A.D.V.S. Appointed executive V.O. to 37th Divl Train. Received orders to discard all surplus equipment and to be prepared to move at 3 hours notice at any time the Division having gone into G.H.Q. reserve at 6 a.m. this day.	A.A.P.
"	5.7.16		Checked all equipment & discarded all surpluses. Overhauled transport vehicles & prepared for prolonged marching. Had all section horses shod up. Attended shoeing board at 37th Divl Train at 2 p.m. & then inspected Hdqrs Coy & Nos 2 & 4 companies. Party to LARBRET station at 8 p.m. to collect head collars from 148 incoming remounts. Party did not return until 3 a.m.	A.A.P.
"	6.7.16		Visited Hdqr. Coy. & No 2 Company & inspected all remounts for 37th Divl. Train. Met A.D.V.S. at WARLINCOURT who informed me that instructions had been received the previous evening to dispatch all the Divisional Infantry to other divisions. This means that forthwith 110th, 111th & 112th Infantry Brigades leave the division and are to be replaced by the remains of 102nd Bde & 103rd Bde of 34th Divn & the 63rd Bde of 21st Divn	

Instructions regarding War Diaries and Intelligence Summaries are contained in F. S. Regs., Part II. and the Staff Manual respectively. Title pages will be prepared in manuscript.

WAR DIARY
or
INTELLIGENCE SUMMARY.
(Erase heading not required.)

Army Form C. 2118.

28 MOBILE SECTION - ARMY VETERINARY CORPS. 37th Divn.

Place	Date	Hour	Summary of Events and Information	Remarks and references to Appendices
GRINCOURT	6.7.16		These units are said to have suffered severely during the recent fighting. Further the Divisional R.A. have changed guns with 46th Division. Hence it would appear that some time must elapse before the 37th Division is reorganised & capable of going into the line again. Preparing for evacuation	A.A.P.
"	7.7.16		Morning preparing weekly returns. Afternoon visited Divl Train, thence to railhead to evacuate 11 horses & mules & on to weekly conference at A.D.V.S' office at PAS.	A.A.P.
"	8.8.16		Met A.D.V.S at 8 a.m. with O.C. Divl Train & inspected 231 and 232 Company A.S.C. which have arrived from 24th Divn to replace our own No 3 & 4 companies which have left the Division. Morning office & sick lines & then to PAS & FAMECHON to search for a mule which had been left behind by 23rd Northumberland Fusiliers. Was unable to find it. Afternoon to Divnl Train. D.D.V.S 3rd Army visited section	A.A.P.
	9.8.16		Sick lines & office & to Divl Train both in morning & afternoon inspecting 231 232 & 63rd Bde Coys A.S.C. who are to rejoin their former divisions.	A.A.P.
	10.8.16		Morning sick lines & office. Men cleaning billets & re-arranging accomodation. At 2 p.m. to NAOURS to collect a horse left by 5th Northamptons. This was a journey of 18 miles each way & orders to do this were received from D.D.V.S. Reserve Army. Returned at 10 p.m. with horse & then to 231 Coy A.S.C. to see a sick horse	A.A.P.
	11.8.16		Morning sick lines & office. Preparing for evacuation next day. Afternoon visited Divl Train & 49th Field Amb.	A.A.P.

T2134. Wt. W708—776. 500000. 4/15. Sir J. C. & S.

Instructions regarding War Diaries and Intelligence Summaries are contained in F. S. Regs., Part II. and the Staff Manual respectively. Title pages will be prepared in manuscript.

WAR DIARY
or
INTELLIGENCE SUMMARY.
(Erase heading not required.)

Army Form C. 2118.

-28 MOBILE SECTION- 37th Divn ARMY VETERINARY CORPS.

Place	Date	Hour	Summary of Events and Information	Remarks and references to Appendices
GRINCOURT	12.7.16		Morning sick lines & office. Afternoon to LARBRET to evacuate 16 animals. Thence to Divl Train.	A.A.P.
"	13.7.16		Morning sick lines & office. A.D.V.S visited section. No 3 Coy 21st Divl Train left the area at noon to rejoin their own Division. Visited Divl Train & 49th Field Ambulance in afternoon & evening.	A.A.P.
"	14.7.16		Visited Divl Train at 7 a.m. Morning sick lines, office & preparing weekly returns. Afternoon to weekly conference at A.D.V.S office. Received preliminary instructions to stand to to march to join 4th Corps 1st Army. Prepared for evacuation next day & commenced loading transport	A.A.P.
	15.7.16		Visited Divl. Train at 6 a.m. Evacuated 24 horses from LARBRET. Handed over billet & field hospital to 1/1st London M.V.S. Marched out at 6 p.m. & proceeded 14 miles in a N.W. direction to BROUILLY arriving 10 p.m. Billeted in the chateau there.	A.A.P.
BROUILLY	16.7.16		Marched from BROUILLY at 12.45 p.m. & proceeding via AMBRINES & SAVY arrived at CAUCOURT at 9 p.m. Bivouaced in an open field. Weather stormy & men & horses experienced considerable discomfort. Accomodation very limited owing to the 2nd Division staff being in the area. Prepared camp & turned in at 12.30 a.m.	A.A.P.
CAUCOURT	17.7.16		Received notification of horses left behind on the march up. Arranged for watering horses & did anything possible to increase the comfort of men & horses. In afternoon visited 2nd Divn M.V.S. to see it with a view to taking over should it move out. It is located at FRESNICOURT.	A.A.P.

T2134. Wt. W708–776. 500000. 4/15. Sir J. C. & S.

Instructions regarding War Diaries and Intelligence Summaries are contained in F. S. Regs., Part II. and the Staff Manual respectively. Title pages will be prepared in manuscript.

WAR DIARY
or
INTELLIGENCE SUMMARY.
(Erase heading not required.)

-28 MOBILE SECTION- 37th Div. ARMY VETERINARY CORPS.

Army Form C. 2118.

Place	Date	Hour	Summary of Events and Information	Remarks and references to Appendices
CAUCOURT	18/7/16		Morning lines & office. Afternoon to search for more suitable billet for section.	AAP
"	19/7/16		Morning to FRESNICOURT to find that 47th Div MVS have taken over the billet there. In afternoon to Div HdQrs at BRYAS & to see an animal of 103rd Bde Machine Gun Coy which had been left behind at ORLENCOURT.	AAP
	20/7/16		Under orders received from RA HdQrs was ordered to move to HERMIN on 21/7/16. In afternoon to Div HdQrs at LE COMTÉ & viewed possible billet at BEUGIN.	AAP
	21/7/16		Sent advanced party to HERMIN and section marched there at 2pm. Prepared	
HERMIN		2pm	camp & admitted some sick. ADVS visited camp in evening & gave orders to move to BEUGIN.	AAP
	22/7/16		Arranged for waggons to take equipment in order that float could be used for sick animals.	
BEUGIN		3.30pm	Arrived at BEUGIN. Experienced much difficulty in securing accommodation as inhabitants were distinctly unfriendly. Rode to D.H.Q. to get an interpreter who came & was of assistance. Move completed with the exception of 2 men & 4 horses who have been left at HERMIN & will require the float tomorrow.	AAP
"	23/7/16		Float made 2 journeys to HERMIN & move was completed. Men engaged in cleaning billets & existing stabling & disinfecting the latter with blow lamp & cresyl.	
"	24/7/16		A.D.V.S. visited section at 9.30am to inspect 3 suspected cases of contagious equine influenza which	

T2134. Wt. W708–776. 500000. 4/15. Sir J. C. & S.

Instructions regarding War Diaries and Intelligence Summaries are contained in F. S. Regs., Part II. and the Staff Manual respectively. Title pages will be prepared in manuscript.

WAR DIARY
or
~~INTELLIGENCE~~ SUMMARY.
(Erase heading not required.)

Army Form C. 2118.

Place	Date	Hour	Summary of Events and Information	Remarks and references to Appendices
BEUGIN	24-7-16		I had reported the previous day. He informed me that 37th Divn was relieving 44th Divn, move to be completed by 29th inst. Got into communication with O.C. 44th Divn M.V.S. with a view to taking over the FRESNICOURT billet. Thence with collecting party to ORLENCOURT and CHELERS. 1 Horse collected. In afternoon preparing for evacuation next day. In evening rode to railhead at BRUAY with a view to securing trucks & forage for the journey.	
"	25-7-16		Received intimation that SE 2555 Pte TUCKER F.E. was invalided to England on 17/7/16 & so becomes struck off the strength. 16 animals evacuated from BRUAY at noon	A.A.V.
"	26-7-16		With conducting party to AMBRINES and ETREE-WAMIN. Two animals collected involving a journey of over 60 kilometres. 7 animals admitted. Received orders to move to FRESNICOURT by 28th inst	A.A.V.
"	27-7-16		Morning sick lines to Field Cashiers Office & to FRESNICOURT to see O.C. 44th Div M.V.S to arrange for taking over tomorrow. Thence to 288 Coy A.S.C. to borrow two waggons & on to A.D.V.S. office to report	A.A.V.
"	28-7-16	7a.m.	Reveille at 4.30 a.m. Breakfast 6.45 & all sick horses marched at 8a.m. Transport at 9a.m.	A.A.V.
FRESNICOURT		noon	Move completed by noon. The billets taken over are stabling erected by the French & which have become an allotted mobile section billet under instructions from 1st Army	

T2134. Wt. W708-776. 500000. 4/15. Sir J. C. & S.

Instructions regarding War Diaries and Intelligence Summaries are contained in F. S. Regs., Part II. and the Staff Manual respectively. Title pages will be prepared in manuscript.

WAR DIARY
~~or~~
~~INTELLIGENCE~~ SUMMARY.
(*Erase heading not required.*)

Army Form C. 2118.

Place	Date	Hour	Summary of Events and Information	Remarks and references to Appendices
FRESNICOURT	28-7-16		There is stabling in a 3 acre paddock for 70 horses & the place is well laid out but standings are in bad repair. The 47th Div left 30 sick behind them which with the 20 from our own Division leaves too many on hand. Consequently communicated with BARLIN which is now railhead & prepared for evacuation next day. On arrival at noon the pump which provided the only water supply for horses from the hospital & two other units was found to be not working. This caused considerable delay, the mid-day watering taking 2½ hours for 75 horses. Consequently I purchased 2 large beer barrels from the inhabitants & placing them on a half limber sent it a mile away to the river & thus filled a hastily contrived trough from a waggon cover. An arduous proceeding but satisfactory as it brought water into the paddock & thus obviated using a trough in common with other units which in my experience is a most unsatisfactory procedure for a Mobile Section. Paid NCO's & men in evening & then turned them on to making bivouacs. To make the place a first class mobile section billet, a cook house, forge, office, pharmacy & mens billet must be built. If we are to be permitted to remain here for any length of time I hope to get this done. Something also must be done to improve the water supply.	A.A.P.

T2134. Wt. W708–776. 500000. 4/15. Sir J. C. & S.

Instructions regarding War Diaries and Intelligence Summaries are contained in F. S. Regs., Part II. and the Staff Manual respectively. Title Pages will be prepared in manuscript.

WAR DIARY or INTELLIGENCE SUMMARY

(Erase heading not required.)

-28 MOBILE SECTION- ARMY VETERINARY CORPS. 37th Divn

Army Form C. 2118

Place	Date	Hour	Summary of Events and Information	Remarks and references to Appendices
FRESNICOURT	29.7.16		37 Horses & mules evacuated at noon including 2 float cases. Very short of water.	AAP
	30.7.16		8 Animals evacuated including 1 float cases. Weather brilliant & oppressively hot. ADVS. visited section	AAP
	31.7.16		Float made journies to MONT St. ELOY & GAUCHIN LEGAL. Agitated for improvement in water supply. Also demanded tents for the men which do not appear to be available. Indented for bricks, paint & other R.E. stores which are urgently required to improve stabling.	AAP
			A.A. Pryer Capt. A.V.C. O.C. 28th Mobile Veterinary Section 37th Division	

1875 Wt. W593/826 1,000,000 4/15 J.B.C. & A. A.D.S.S./Forms/C. 2118.

Instructions regarding War Diaries and Intelligence Summaries are contained in F. S. Regs., Part II. and the Staff Manual respectively. Title Pages will be prepared in manuscript.

WAR DIARY
or
INTELLIGENCE SUMMARY
(Erase heading not required.)

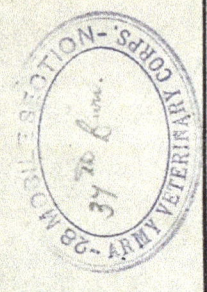

28 MOBILE SECTION - ARMY VETERINARY CORPS. 37th Divn.

Army Form C. 2118

Vol 11

Place	Date	Hour	Summary of Events and Information	Remarks and references to Appendices
FRESNICOURT	1.8.16		37 Animals evacuated making a total of 82 in five days which is very heavy work considering the difficulties as to shortness of water & men & the distance from railhead. Men employed in repairing stabling etc.	A.A.P.
"	2.8.16		Usual section work. Water fatigues. erecting cook houses & new latrines	A.A.P.
"	3.8.16		Waggon to ESTREE-CAUCHIE to fetch 2 waggon covers & 3 tents for men. Made mange kraal.	A.A.P.
"	4.8.16		14 Animals evacuated. Requested IVth Corps to supply a water trough & installation. Fenced off paddock & prepared an office.	A.A.P.
"	5.8.16		Usual section work. A.D.V.S. visited section. Started to build forge & an oven. 14 Animals evacuated.	A.A.P.
"	6.8.16		Usual section work. Rode round portion of Divisional Area in evening to acquaint myself with position of waggon lines & 1st Line transport.	A.A.P.
"	7.8.16		Village well repaired enabling water to be obtained somewhat more quickly although it still has to be drawn in barrels & conveyed to the lines on a half limber. Preparing for evacuation next day	A.A.P.
"	8.8.16		17 Animals evacuated. Many admissions to prepare for another evacuation.	A.A.P.
"	9.8.16		26 Animals evacuated. Shaft of ambulance broken necessitating sending the vehicle to Ordnance Workshops for repairs. The disadvantages of such a vehicle being of no recognised pattern are very evident as in this case for a new shaft will have to be made entailing much delay before it can be used again	A.A.P.
"	10.8.16		Morning sick lines & office. A.D.V.S. visited section & informed me that the 9th Division would probably relieve 37th Divn. at an early date and the 37th Divn will go into Corps Reserve in the Area vacated by 9th Divn. In afternoon to Field Cashiers office & rode round new area in search for suitable billet. Do not think we shall be able to do better that exchange with 21st M.V.S. 9th Divn which is at BRUAY. In evening paid NCO's & men.	A.A.P.
"	11.8.16		Morning sick lines & office. Afternoon to weekly conference at A.D.V.S. office at CAMBLAIN L'ABBÉ	

1875 Wt. W593/826 1,000,000 4/15 J.B.C. & A. A.D.S.S./Forms/C. 2118.

Instructions regarding War Diaries and Intelligence Summaries are contained in F. S. Regs., Part II. and the Staff Manual respectively. Title Pages will be prepared in manuscript.

WAR DIARY
or
INTELLIGENCE SUMMARY
(Erase heading not required.)

-28 MOBILE SECTION- ARMY VETERINARY CORPS. 37th Divn.

Army Form C. 2118

Place	Date	Hour	Summary of Events and Information	Remarks and references to Appendices
FRESNICOURT	11.8.16		Here I received instructions for the move to BRUAY to take place on 16th prox. Also Major PALLIN informed me that he would probably be leaving the Division shortly on appointment to a DDVS & temp. Lt. Colonel. This I much regretted to hear. He believed that his successor was to be Major J. R. STEEVENSON	A.A.P.
"	12.8.16		Morning sick lines & office. Afternoon to COUIGNY at request of French mission 4th Corps to see sick horse belonging to French farmer. Evening office. Got float back from Ordnance Workshops.	A.A.P.
"	13.8.16		Sick lines & office. Summoned to CAMBLAIN L'ABBÉ at noon where Major PALLIN informed me that he was leaving at 2 p.m. for BOULOGNE to take up the appointment of D.D.V.S. Northern. He called at the section on his way, making a final inspection & bidding farewell to the N.C.O.'s & men on parade. Wire from D.V.S. arrived instructing me to officiate as A.D.V.S. 37th Divn until a successor to Major PALLIN was appointed. Preparing for evacuation next day	A.A.P.
"	14.8.16		Morning sick lines & office & to BARLIN station to evacuate 26 animals including two float cases. Then on to abattoir to see horse destroyed. Afternoon to CAMBLAIN L'ABBE.	A.A.P.
"	15.8.16		Preparing to move to BRUAY next day. Ambulance to GAUCHIN-L-Gal at reveille. My groom SE 6164 Pte BARNES J. evacuated sick. Preparing for another evacuation next day. To 9th Div. M.V.S. in afternoon to make final preparations for taking over. Then to D.H.Q. who have moved to BRUAY & arranged for A.D.V.S. office. Was informed by Q office that 37th Divl. R.A. would move to join VIth Corps 3rd Army on 14th inst. Sent advanced party to BRUAY to take over.	A.A.P.
"	16.8.16		Returned tents to Town Major ESTREE-CAUCHIE at reveille. Find that new billet is in the commune of LABUISSIÉRE & not in BRUAY. Left FRESNICOURT at 10.30 with convoy of sick. Thence to BARLIN where we halted & entrained 9 animals. Thence to HAILLICOURT - BRUAY to new billets at LABUISSIERE arriving 2.30 p.m. Spent remainder of day in preparing camp. Vicinity of camp bombed by hostile aircraft at 11 p.m. No casualties	A.A.P.
LABUISSIERE		2.30 p.m.		
"	17.8.16		Morning sick lines & office & away on A.D.V.S. duties. Evening office	A.A.P.

1875 Wt. W593/826 1,000,000 4/15 J.B.C. & A. A.D.S.S./Forms/C. 2118.

Instructions regarding War Diaries and Intelligence Summaries are contained in F. S. Regs., Part II. and the Staff Manual respectively. Title Pages will be prepared in manuscript.

WAR DIARY
or
INTELLIGENCE SUMMARY
(Erase heading not required.)

-28 MOBILE SECTION- 37th Divn ARMY VETERINARY CORPS.

Army Form C. 2118

Place	Date	Hour	Summary of Events and Information	Remarks and references to Appendices
LABUISSIERE	18.8.16		Morning sick lines & office. Visited 50th Field Amb. as executive V.O. Afternoon & evening A.D.V.S. duties. Very heavy rain causing much discomfort to men who have no adequate cover.	A.A.P.
"	19.8.16		Continued rain. Secured a room for use as a cook house & mess room for the men who up till the present have been cooking in the open. Office & sick lines. A.D.V.S. duties occupied the greater portion of the day.	A.A.P.
"	20.8.16		Morning sick lines & office. A.D.V.S. duties for remainder of the day.	A.A.P.
"	21.8.16		Morning sick lines & office. A.D.V.S. duties remainder of the day. D.D.V.S 1st Army visited section at 2.30 p.m.	A.A.P.
"	22.8.16		Morning office & A.D.V.S. duties. Afternoon sick lines. Evening A.D.V.S. duties. S.E 1063 Pte BREEDS. C joined for duty from No1 Convalescent Horse Depot.	A.A.P.
"	23.8.16		Morning sick lines & office. Afternoon & evening A.D.V.S. duties.	A.A.P.
"	24.8.16		A.D.V.S. duties before breakfast. Morning sick lines & office. 25 remounts received for distribution. Visited Field Cashiers Office & paid N.C.O.'s & men	A.A.P.
"	25.8.16		Morning sick lines & office. Then to Q office & with O.C. Train to inspect 13th Royal Fusiliers, 13th K.R.R. & 111th Machine Gun Company. 10 Animals evacuated from BRUAY. Afternoon & evening A.D.V.S. duties	A.A.P.
"	26.8.16		Morning rifle & smoke helmet inspection. Then to inspect 13th Rifle Bde & 10th Royal Fusiliers. Afternoon A.D.V.S. office & A.D.V.S. At 9.15 p.m. 6724 Sergt FLOOD was reported as drunk by the Orderly NCO. 4986 Corpl LAMBERT. Two warrant officers from 8th M.A.C. stated the accused was perfectly sober & accordingly he was not placed in arrest.	A.A.P.
"	27.8.16		Held enquiry into the circumstances under which Corpl LAMBERT ~~reported~~ Sergt. FLOOD as being drunk. No satisfactory evidence forthcoming but circumstances point to the action being a purely malicious one. Censured Corpl LAMBERT but was unable to take further action owing to lack of evidence.	

1875 Wt. W593/826 1,000,000 4/15 J.B.C. & A. A.F.S.S./Forms/C. 2118.

Instructions regarding War Diaries and Intelligence Summaries are contained in F. S. Regs., Part II. and the Staff Manual respectively. Title Pages will be prepared in manuscript.

WAR DIARY
or
INTELLIGENCE SUMMARY
(Erase heading not required.)

Army Form C. 2118

Place	Date	Hour	Summary of Events and Information	Remarks and references to Appendices
BRUAY	27.8.16		Having noticed during the past week that the NCO's & men of the section are not working with that cohesion which is necessary for efficiency I warned the section on parade that henceforward the standard of discipline demanded would be much higher & any breach would would met with the maximum punishment. Few of the men who formed the original section give any trouble but the reinforcements are not such good men. In spite of instructions from the D.V.S. that only young well conducted men are to be sent to Mobile Sections men frequently join with many serious offences on the conduct sheets. They are often too old lazy & confirmed grumblers & evidently soldiers that no one wishes to have under their command. The result of having such men in a small unit with only one officer & a percentage of NCO's of doubtful value is easily seen.	A.A.P.
"	28.8.16		Handed over A.D.V.S. duties to Major J. R. STEEVENSON. A.V.C. who arrived from No 14 Veterinary Hospital the previous evening. Visited 50th Field Amb. & 37th Divl Signal Coy.	A.A.P.
"	29.8.16		Morning sick lines & office. Afternoon visited D.H.Q. horses. Evening to A.D.V.S. office. Very heavy rain completely flooding standings & bivouacs.	A.A.P.
"	30.8.16		Continued heavy rain. Morning sick lines & office. A.D.V.S. visited section. Afternoon sick lines & office.	A.A.P.
"	31.8.16.		Improved weather. Morning sick lines & office & estimated requirements for material to repair billets & stables & forwarded indent for same to C.R.E. Afternoon with A.D.V.S. to visit Echelon B. 37th Divl Column at HOUVELIN.	A.A.P.

A.A. Pryer
Captain A.V.C.
O.C. 28th Mobile Veterinary Section
37th Division

1875 Wt. W593/826 1,000,000 4/15 J.B.C. & A. A.D.S.S./Forms/C. 2118.

Vol 12

WAR DIARY Sept 1916

28th Mob. Vet. Section

37th Divn

Instructions regarding War Diaries and Intelligence Summaries are contained in F. S. Regs., Part II. and the Staff Manual respectively. Title Pages will be prepared in manuscript.

WAR DIARY
or
INTELLIGENCE SUMMARY
(Erase heading not required.)

Army Form C. 2118

Place	Date	Hour	Summary of Events and Information	Remarks and references to Appendices
LABUISSIERE	1.9.16		Morning sick lines & office. A.D.V.S. visited section 7 animals evacuated. Visited 50th Field Ambulance. To conference at A.D.V.S. office in afternoon. Seven section men lodged frivolous complaints & asked to be re posted.	A.A.P.
"	2.9.16		R E commenced repairing stables & billets assisted by fatigue party from the section. Refused re posting to those men who made the requests. A.D.M.S 37th Div inspected stables & billets	A.A.P.
"	3.9.16		Morning parade church service. Fatigue parties carting material for standings. Secured six tents & moved men from present billets in a dark loft into them. Heavy rain in evening	A.A.P.
"	4.9.16		Continued rain & rough weather. Sick lines office & visited 50th Field Ambulance.	A.A.P.
"	5.9.16		Received material from R.E. & continued building & repairing stables & billets. Continued rain.	A.A.P.
"	6.9.16		Improved weather. Visited 50th Field Amb. A.D.V.S. visited section. Continued work on buildings etc. To BOURS in afternoon to collect a horse.	A.A.P.
"	7.9.16		5 Animals evacuated. Work continued. Sick lines & office. With A.D.V.S. to OURTON in afternoon. Paid NCO's & men	A.A.P.
"	8.9.16		Morning sick lines & office. Ambulance to DIVION. A.D.V.S. visited section. Men working on stables & billets. 15 loads of red slag carted for making standings.	A.A.P.
"	9.9.16		Morning sick lines & office. Building continued. A quiet day.	A.A.P.
"	10.9.16		Parade church service 9.15 a.m. Morning to 50th Field Ambulance. Afternoon sick lines & office.	A.A.P.
"	11.9.16		Morning sick lines & office. A.D.V.S. visited section. Building continued. Afternoon limber to Divisional Laundry for clean underclothing. Weather dull	A.A.P.
"	12.9.16		Morning sick lines & office. Afternoon to 21st M.V.S. 9th Div. at FRESNICOURT.	A.A.P.
"	13.9.16		To railhead at 8 a.m. to inspect & distribute remounts. 1 horse destroyed & sold for 100 francs at 9 a.m. Morning sick lines & office & preparing for evacuation next day. A.D.V.S. visited section. In afternoon to BEAUMETZ-lez-AIRE with a view to collecting four horses. On arrival found that they had been collected by an unknown unit on the previous Friday so had the journey for nothing.	A.A.P.

1875 Wt. W593/826 1,000,000 4/15 J.B.C. & A. A.D.S.S./Forms/C. 2118.

Instructions regarding War Diaries and Intelligence Summaries are contained in F. S. Regs., Part II. and the Staff Manual respectively. Title Pages will be prepared in manuscript.

WAR DIARY
or
INTELLIGENCE SUMMARY
(Erase heading not required.)

Army Form C. 2118

28 MOBILE SECTION ARMY VETERINARY CORPS — 37th Divn

Place	Date	Hour	Summary of Events and Information	Remarks and references to Appendices
LABUISSIERE	14.9.16		Morning sick lines & office. A.D.V.S visited section. To 50th Field Ambulance & to railhead to see seven animals evacuated. S.E. 6724 Sergt. FLOOD P.F. sent to No 12 Veterinary Hospital for a course of instruction in clipping & care of the Stewart Clipping Machine	AAP
"	15.9.16		Morning sick lines & office. A.D.V.S. visited section. Prepared weekly returns. Afternoon sick lines & office	AAP
"	16.9.16		37th Divisional Artillery returned into Divisional Area from 35th Divn. Usual section work	AAP
"	17.9.16		Morning sick lines & office. Church parade at 9.15 a.m. Then left with A.D.V.S. & spent the day inspecting the Divnl R.A. at LA THIEULOYE, MAGNICOURT and HOUVELIN. Received preliminary instructions that the 37th Divn would relieve 63rd Royal Naval Division. Move to be completed by 19th inst. This will probably mean taking over the billets of 53rd Mobile Veterinary Section.	AAP
"	18.9.16		Morning sick lines & office. Preparing for evacuation next day & for moving. In evening to 53rd M.V.S. at BARLIN. Consider it a very poor billet. Heavy rain all day so perhaps it was seen under unfavourable circumstances. Arranged to move in on Wednesday morning. Float to OURTON.	AAP
"	19.9.16		Morning sick lines & office. Very heavy rain. Preparing to move next morning	AAP
"	20.9.16		Continued heavy rain. Struck camp & loaded waggons before breakfast. Marched from LABUISSIERE at 9 a.m.	
BARLIN		10.30 a.m.	Arrived & found 53rd M.V.S. had not departed. They eventually left later in the day. Spent day in preparing camp.	AAP
"	21.9.16		Ambulance to BAJUS. Further rain. 7 Cases admitted. Work done in draining & improving stables & billets.	AAP
"	22.9.16		Improved weather. Usual section work. Preparing for evacuation next day. SE 14834 S.S. CLARK J. joined from No 14 Veterinary Hospital	AAP

1875 Wt. W593/826 1,000,000 4/15 J.B.C. & A. A.D.S.S./Forms/C. 2118.

Instructions regarding War Diaries and Intelligence Summaries are contained in F. S. Regs., Part II. and the Staff Manual respectively. Title Pages will be prepared in manuscript.

WAR DIARY
or
INTELLIGENCE SUMMARY
(Erase heading not required.)

Army Form C. 2118

Place	Date	Hour	Summary of Events and Information	Remarks and references to Appendices
BARLIN	23.9.16		Morning sick lines. 17 Animals evacuated. Afternoon office. SE 5619 Corpl. S.S. BROWN. H.B transferred to No 14 Veterinary Hospital ABBEVILLE.	A.A.P.
"	24.9.16		Church parade 10 a.m. Morning sick lines & office. Weather very good. Afternoon inspected section transport & arranged for vehicles & harness to be sent to 288 Coy. ASC next morning for overhauling & necessary repairs	A.A.P.
"	25.9.16		Preparing for evacuation next day. Lorry to COUPIGNY for RE material. Usual section work. SE 4936 Corpl LAMBERT S.A.N. evacuated sick.	A.A.P.
"	26.9.16		12 Animals evacuated. Eight animals admitted. Preparing indents for winter clothing and painting vehicles. To 24th Div M.V.S at FRESNICOURT in afternoon.	A.A.P.
"	27.9.16		Kit inspection at 9 a.m. Usual section work	A.A.P.
"	28.9.16		Usual section work	A.A.P.
"	29.9.16		Fatigue party with lorries carting slag for standings from FOSSE 5. Preparing for evacuation next day. Afternoon to weekly conference at A.D.V.S. office	A.A.P.
"	30.9.16		Slag fatigues continued. 15 Animals evacuated. Ambulance to BRACQUEMCOURT. Weather fine but cooler.	A.A.P.

A.A. Pryor [signature]
Capt. AVC.
O.C. 28th Mobile Veterinary Section

1875 Wt. W593/826 1,000,000 4/15 J.B.C. & A. A.D.S.S./Forms/C. 2118.

Instructions regarding War Diaries and Intelligence Summaries are contained in F. S. Regs., Part II. and the Staff Manual respectively. Title Pages will be prepared in manuscript.

WAR DIARY
or
INTELLIGENCE SUMMARY
(Erase heading not required.)

28 MOBILE SECTION ARMY VETERINARY CORPS 37th Divn

Army Form C. 2118

Vol 13

Place	Date	Hour	Summary of Events and Information	Remarks and references to Appendices
BARLIN	1.10.16		Parade C of E service 10 a m. One horse destroyed and sold for butchery. Weather dull & cooler.	AAP
"	2.10.16		Fatigue party loading slag. Work on billets continued. Heavy rain. Usual section work	AAP
"	3.10.16		Work & fatigues as yesterday. Preparing for evacuation next day. Ambulance to BOIS D'OLHAIN. To Field Cashier in afternoon.	AAP
"	4.10.16		Continued heavy rain. New cook house completed. 18 Animals evacuated. Ambulance to BOIS D'OLHAIN - one horse sold for butchery	AAP
"	5.10.16		Usual section work. Two float cases collected. Fatigue party loading slag & men at work on renovating stables. Paid NCO's & men	AAP
"	6.10.16		Usual section work. Two serious cases cast for dressing & urgent operation. Continued rain. To weekly conference of V.O's in afternoon.	AAP
"	7.10.16		Usual section work. Commenced clipping section horses. Men making roads & standings.	AAP
"	8.10.16		Parade C of E service. Men cleaning harness in afternoon. Held Court of Enquiry as to the manner in which SE 4936 P/A/Corpl LAMBERT sustained an injury to his knee. President Capt. A.A PRYER AVC Members Capt W. HUSTON AVC and Capt. J WADDELL AVC	AAP
"	9.10.16		Usual section work. Morning sick lines & office. Afternoon fatigues. Weather warmer & brighter.	AAP
"	10.10.16		Morning sick lines & office & then with ADVS to inspect C/125 & C/123 R.F.A. Afternoon sick lines.	AAP
"	11.10.16		Morning sick lines & office. 16 Animals evacuated. In afternoon to DIVION to inspect 4th Corps Cavalry Regiment.	AAP

1875 Wt. W593/826 1.000,000 4/15 J.B.C. & A. A.D.S.S./Forms/C. 2118.

Instructions regarding War Diaries and Intelligence Summaries are contained in F. S. Regs., Part II. and the Staff Manual respectively. Title Pages will be prepared in manuscript.

WAR DIARY
or
INTELLIGENCE SUMMARY
(Erase heading not required.)

Army Form C. 2118

Place	Date	Hour	Summary of Events and Information	Remarks and references to Appendices
BARLIN	12.10.16		Morning collecting party to DIVION. Ambulance to 4th Corps Cavalry at DIVION making two journies. Attended gas course for instruction in small box respirator at Divisional Gas School at BOEFFLES in afternoon. 18 cases admitted. SE 963 Pte BOURNE F. joined from No 6 Veterinary Hospital.	A.A.P.
"	13.10.16		Sent NCO to Divisional Gas School in morning. 26 animals evacuated. Received preliminary orders that 37th Division is to proceed into 1st Army Reserve upon being relieved by 2nd Canadian Division. Relief to be completed by 10am on 18th inst. Accordingly began to	A.A.P.
"	14.10.16		check equipment with a view to moving with transport lightly loaded. Usual section work. Heavy rain.	A.A.P.
"	15.10.16		To railhead at 8am to inspect 123 incoming remounts & to collect head collars from same. Ambulance to BOEFFLES. Section inspected by DDVS 1st Army & DDR 1st Army in afternoon. Received orders that the section was to march out at 9.30am with DHQ to ROELLCOURT. Owing to the fact that this would take me a long way from the RA & most of the horsed units where we should be of most use the matter was laid before the General Staff who cancelled the order & intimated that the move should be carried out under orders of the B.G.R.A. which should prove more satisfactory. We shall now move in conjunction with Hdqrs Coy 37th Divl Train	A.A.P.
"	16.10.16		To BURBURE and RAIMBERT in morning to collect a horse left behind by 9th Canadian F.A. Was unable to trace the animal & reported accordingly. Afternoon preparing for evacuation next day.	
	17.10.16		Owing to the number of sick arranged with Staff Captain R.A. to move on 18th inst instead of 17th inst. 22 animals evacuated. Afternoon loading limbers. To field cashier at HERSIN. Paid NCOs & men	A.A.P.
	18.10.16		Relieved by M.V.S of 2nd Canadian Division at 8.30am. Marched out into 1st Army Reserve Area at 9.20am. Proceeded via HAILLICOURT, BRUAY, DIVION, DIEVAL and BOURS to MAREST	

1875 Wt. W593/826 1,000,000 4/15 J.B.C. & A. A.D.S.S./Forms/C. 2118.

Army Form C. 2118.

Instructions regarding War Diaries and Intelligence Summaries are contained in F. S. Regs., Part II. and the Staff Manual respectively. Title Pages will be prepared in manuscript.

WAR DIARY
or
~~INTELLIGENCE SUMMARY~~
(Erase heading not required.)

28 MOBILE SECTION — ARMY VETERINARY CORPS. 34th Div.

Place	Date	Hour	Summary of Events and Information	Remarks and references to Appendices
MAREST	18.10.16	2.20pm	Arrived at MAREST. Considerable delay was caused owing to the ambulance being bogged at DIEVAL necessitating unloading & reloading it. Erected lines & bivouaced in open field. Weather wet & cold.	AAP
"	19.10.16		Very heavy rain all night & all day. Horse lines & men's bivouacs under water. In afternoon to R.A. Hdqrs. at PERNES & got operation orders for next day & issued necessary instructions for moving.	AAP
" OSTREVILLE	20.10.16		Marched from MAREST 8.15am. Roads very bad necessitating use of drag ropes. Marched via BOURS, ANTIN, BRYAS to OSTREVILLE arriving 11.30am. Got all men & horses under cover. Refilled at 8am & 4pm. Weather bright but cold.	AAP
ETREE-WAMIN	21.10.16		Marched from OSTREVILLE at 8.30am & proceeded via MARQUAY & TINQUES to LINGEREUIL. Halted watered & fed. Then on to LIENCOURT & to ETREE-WAMIN. Bivouaced for the night & prepared to move at 7a.m. next morning in accordance with Divl Artillery Operation Order No 30.	AAP
ORVILLE	22.10.16		Left ETREE-WAMIN at 7am & proceeded via REBREUVE, BOQUEMAISON & DOULLENS to destination at AUTHIEUL. There found that we were to go on to ORVILLE owing to the congestion of troops. Arrived ORVILLE 2pm. Horse lines very crowded & bad. Spent remainder of day in searching for accommodation for men. Was successful at last & got them all in a warm dry loft.	AAP
"	23.10.16		Rested at ORVILLE. Drew tents & bivouacs. A.D.V.S. visited me in morning & instructed me to report at D.H.Q. at 2p.m. for orders. Reported accordingly & was instructed to stand fast & await further orders. Weather very bad. Hdqrs. of 34th Divl Train moved further on leaving me behind. At present I am functionless owing to lack of room for standings.	AAP
"	24.10.16		Went in morning to Town Majors Office to obtain better accommodation. After much difficulty obtained a dilapidated barn for 60 horses. Spent afternoon in changing into new site. Very heavy rain.	
		11pm	Received orders from 34th R.A. to be clear of all billets by 8am. next day to make room for 8th Divl Artillery. This leaves me without instruction as to where to go.	AAP

2449 Wt. W14957/M90 750,000 1/16 J.B.C. & A. Forms/C.2118/12.

Army Form C. 2118.

Instructions regarding War Diaries and Intelligence Summaries are contained in F. S. Regs., Part II. and the Staff Manual respectively. Title pages will be prepared in manuscript.

WAR DIARY
or
~~INTELLIGENCE SUMMARY.~~
(*Erase heading not required.*)

28 MOBILE SECTION - ARMY VETERINARY CORPS. 37th Divn

Place	Date	Hour	Summary of Events and Information	Remarks and references to Appendices
ORVILLE	25.10.16		To D.H.Q. at [illegible] to ask for instructions as to where to go. Was instructed to move into the chateau park at MARIEUX next to D.H.Q. Returned to ORVILLE & marched section to MARIEUX	A.A.P.
MARIEUX		12.30pm	arriving 12.30 p.m. Established camp. Very heavy rain causing great discomfort.	
"	26.10.16		In morning with A.D.V.S. to office of D.D.V.S. Reserve Army & thence to R.A. waggon lines. Then on to find railhead at BELLE EGLISE to make arrangements for trucks & forage. Afternoon preparing for evacuation.	A.A.P.
"	27.10.16		To railhead. 5 animals evacuated. Float busy.	A.A.P.
"	28.10.16		To AMPLIER in morning to collect 4 horses left behind by 8th Divnl Artillery. Afternoon preparing for evacuation.	
"	29.10.16		Morning sick lines & office. To railhead at noon. 14 animals evacuated. Float made two journeys. A very satisfactory days work under difficult conditions.	A.A.P.
"	30.10.16		Very heavy rain. 12 animals admitted. Experienced great difficulty in taking descriptions & preparing for evacuation next day.	A.A.P.
"	31.10.16		19 Animals evacuated. Improved weather conditions. Float made two journies to railhead. Wrote D.A.P.M. 37th Division requesting that the Reserve Army Order requiring all horses to be provided with bits when on the roads & that no man may lead more than one horse mounted or two dismounted might be removed in the case of sick horses to railhead. It is impossible for Mobile Veterinary Section to comply.	A.A.P.

A A Piper
Capt AVC
OC 28th Mobile Veterinary Section

A5834 Wt. W4973/M687 750,000 8/16 D. D. & L. Ltd. Forms/C.2118/13

Instructions regarding War Diaries and Intelligence Summaries are contained in F. S. Regs., Part II. and the Staff Manual respectively. Title pages will be prepared in manuscript.

WAR DIARY
or
INTELLIGENCE SUMMARY.
(Erase heading not required.)

Army Form C. 2118.

Mob Vety Sec 37th Division

8 vol 14

Place	Date	Hour	Summary of Events and Information	Remarks and references to Appendices
MARIEUX	1-11-16		Morning with collecting party to ORVILLE and HEM. Afternoon preparing for evacuation next day.	A.A.P.
"	2-11-16		Very heavy rain. 5 animals evacuated from BELLE EGLISE. Then on to VARENNES junction to inspect & distribute 74 remounts for divisional artillery. Returned 9 pm.	A.A.P.
"	3-11-16		18 animals admitted. Ambulance made 3 journeys. To AMPLIER with collecting party in afternoon to collect 8 horses left behind by N.Z. F.A. Heavy rain.	A.A.P.
"	4-11-16		30 cases admitted mostly from 56th Division. 35 animals evacuated from BELLE EGLISE.	A.A.P.
"	5-11-16		16 animals evacuated from BELLE EGLISE.	A.A.P.
"	6-11-16		Very heavy rain. The site occupied by the section is now almost uninhabitable but there seems no possibility of obtaining authority to move elsewhere to more suitable surroundings. Afternoon with collecting party to AMPLIER.	A.A.P.
"	7-11-16		Continued heavy rain. Preparing for evacuation next day. Paid NCO's & men.	A.A.P.
"	8-11-16		24 animals evacuated from BELLE EGLISE. Collecting party to AMPLIER as usual to collect 10 horses left behind by 41st Division.	A.A.P.
"	9-11-16		To HEM to collect a horse in the morning. Section inspected by D.D.V.S. Fifth Army in afternoon. Preparing for evacuation next day.	A.A.P.
"	10-11-16		25 animals evacuated from BELLE EGLISE. Somewhat improved weather conditions. Evening – office	A.A.P.
"	11-11-16		Usual section work. 4 animals collected from 3rd (R.I.) Bun. at PUCHEVILLERS	A.A.P.
"	12-11-16		24 animals evacuated. 18 admitted in evening. Preparing to evacuate again next day.	A.A.P.
"	13-11-16		25 animals evacuated from BELLE EGLISE	A.A.P.

A5834 Wt. W4973/M687 750,000 8/16 D. D. & L. Ltd. Forms/C.2118/13

Instructions regarding War Diaries and Intelligence Summaries are contained in F. S. Regs., Part II. and the Staff Manual respectively. Title pages will be prepared in manuscript.

WAR DIARY
or
INTELLIGENCE SUMMARY.
(Erase heading not required.)

-98 MOBILE SECTION- ARMY VETERINARY CORPS. 37th Divn

Army Form C. 2118.

Place	Date	Hour	Summary of Events and Information	Remarks and references to Appendices
MARIEUX	14.11.16		Received preliminary instructions to relieve 63rd Division in the line. Preparing for evacuation next day	AAP
"	15.11.16		24 animals evacuated from BELLE EGLISE then on to 63rd M.V.S who were situated on the HEADAUVILLE - ENGLEBELMER road in the open. Received orders to relieve them by 4 pm next day. O.C. 53rd MVS 63rd (R.N.) Divn said he could not move by then so arranged to close up	AAP
HEDAUVILLE	16.11.16		Packed up & marched from MARIEUX at noon. Arrived HEADAUVILLE 3 pm. Found 53rd M.V.S had still over 70 animals to evacuate. Condition very bad	AAP
"	17.11.16		Received instructions to move back to FORCEVILLE to make room for 11th Divn. Went to FORCEVILLE to secure accomodation but got nothing so returned to find 53rd M.V.S moving to ARQUEVES & leaving 83 animals in my charge. These animals were in many cases tied up with wire & only after great difficulty would O.C. 53rd MVS leave O men & a very inadequate supply of forage for them. Obtained authority from 5th Corps to day where I was told these animals could be evacuated. Arranged to evacuate from BELLE EGLISE next day. Heavy snowfall during the night	AAP
"	18.11.16		Capt WHITEHURST sent to ~~[illegible]~~ head as driver for pack transport animals. 75 animals conducted to BELLE EGLISE in storm	
"	19.11.16		75 walking cases evacuated from BELLE EGLISE. A very hard days work	AAP
"	20.11.16		22nd M.V.S 11th Divn arrived & we closed up in the same camp. Owing to the unfavorable condition of the standings walked 16 very bad cases to lines of 1/1st Highland M.V.S at FORCEVILLE & left them there for the night.	
"	21.11.16		16 float cases evacuated from ACHEUX	AAP

A5834 Wt. W4973/M687 750,000 8/16 D. D. & L. Ltd. Forms/C.2118/13

Instructions regarding War Diaries and Intelligence Summaries are contained in F. S. Regs., Part II. and the Staff Manual respectively. Title pages will be prepared in manuscript.

WAR DIARY
or
INTELLIGENCE SUMMARY.
(*Erase heading not required.*)

37th Div.

Army Form C. 2118.

Place	Date	Hour	Summary of Events and Information	Remarks and references to Appendices
HEDAUVILLE	21.11.16		28 animals evacuated from BELLE EGLISE in conjunction with 22nd M.V.S. 11th Div. Roads in very bad condition & traffic very congested rendering movement of convoy very difficult & slow.	A.A.P.
"	22.11.16		Weather very cold. Prepared a small standing with chalk to keep foot cases out of the mud	A.A.P.
"	23.11.16		Received preliminary instructions to move into rest on 25th inst. 25 animals admitted. 22nd M.V.S. left to rejoin 19th Div. at BOUZINCOURT leaving 8 float cases behind. Owing to impending move cannot evacuate these so prepared to transfer all cases to 22nd M.V.S. at BOUZINCOURT next day where they will be evacuated by them from ALBERT. Capt A A PRYER granted special leave to England owing to the death of his father. Temporary command of the section handed over to Capt. J. H YATES V.O. 1/126th Bd. R F A and N.C.O.s & men.	A.A.P.
"	24.11.16		J. H. Yates Captn. A.V.C. took over charge (temporary) of 28th M.V.S. and after usual section duties handed over 31 animals to the 22nd V.M.S. Horse left by same unit previous day died during the night. The weather conditions were bad. Heavy rains.	J.H.Y.
"	25.11.16		Received orders to leave Hedauville and proceed to MARIEUX. The section left 10-45 the climatic conditions were very bad. Raining very heavily. Handed over 5 Tents and 19 Bivouacs to the Town Major. The roads were in very bad condition and ACHEUX had been shelled before we passed through.	J.H.Y.
MARIEUX	26.11.16		Usual section duties. Collected 15 animals. Had the use of a motor ambulance which was of very great service as there were no less than 8 cases which otherwise would have to have been fetched with the horse float. One animal died.	J.H.Y.

Instructions regarding War Diaries and Intelligence Summaries are contained in F. S. Regs., Part II. and the Staff Manual respectively. Title pages will be prepared in manuscript.

WAR DIARY
or
INTELLIGENCE SUMMARY.
(Erase heading not required.)

Army Form C. 2118.

Place	Date	Hour	Summary of Events and Information	Remarks and references to Appendices
MARIEUX.	27.11.16		Usual section duties. Weather conditions improved. Collected 16 animals and evacuated 35. from Belle ESLISE. The motor ambulance was again lent to this section and proved of great service conveying 8 animals to the station + collecting 3. at other points.	J.W.Y.
"	28.11.16		Weather conditions still continue fair. Usual section duties 39 animals were admitted and two collected. A horse was found tied to a telegraph pole and sent in, it was in exceptionally poor condition.	J.W.Y.
"	29.11.16		Usual section duties. 9 animals admitted to the section. Evacuated 49 Horses + 4 Mules from BELLE ESLISE station to ABBERVILLE. The road was in a very bad condition. Had the use of Motor Ambulance which brought in 3 animals and also conveyed animals to the station as well as our own float. The Glasgow Yeomanry lent section 15 mounted men to help to convey walking cases to station.	J.W.Y.
"	30.11.16		Usual section duties. Went to ORVILLE + recovered a horse which had been left with an inhabitant unit unknown, also one horse from the TOWN MAJOR of SARTON. Motor Ambulance brought in 4 animals, and the section ~~own~~ float two. PTE LUTHER was granted leave. Selected site for proposed standings for section. 20. animals were admitted to the section.	

J W Y Yates. Capt AVC.
A/O.C. 28th Mobile Veterinary Section
37. Division.

A5834 Wt. W4973/M687 750,000 8/16 D. D. & L. Ltd. Forms/C.2118/13

28TH
MOBILE VETERINARY
SECTION.
No. V677
Date 31-12-16

37th Divn. "A"

Herewith War Diary for 28th MOBILE VETERINARY SECTION for the month of December 1916.

A. A. Fraser Capt. AVC
O.C. 28th Mob. Vet. Section

31-12-16

Instructions regarding War Diaries and Intelligence Summaries are contained in F. S. Regs., Part II. and the Staff Manual respectively. Title pages will be prepared in manuscript.

WAR DIARY
or
INTELLIGENCE SUMMARY.
(Erase heading not required.)

Army Form C. 2118.

Mob 37 Vety Sect

Vol 15

Place	Date	Hour	Summary of Events and Information	Remarks and references to Appendices
MARIEUX	1-12-16		At present the number of admittances to Section of sick horses approximately less still 21 horses and 4 mules were evacuated from BELLE EGLISE STATION 8 of these being float cases 4 of them being conveyed by the Motor Ambulances. The weather conditions were cold but fine	JHY
"	2-12-16		Most of the evacuations from this Section have been animals from units other than the 37 Division only about 3 per cent of animals from our units. Sgt Flood reported sick, and conveyed to Hospital and received notice that he was evacuated. This Sgt was a very efficient N.C.O. & has been with unit since its formation. Hope section does not permanently loose his services 20 animals were admitted	JHY
"	3-12-16		26 Animals were evacuated by this Section from Belle Eglise. Called at Arqueves and saw horse standings suitable for the section also made arrangements for men's billets + etc The section being under orders to move to ARQUIVES on the 4th inst. Received information that 7 horses of various units were left at AEUTHIEUL. 4 of these were collected today	JHY
ARQUEVES	4-12-16		Moved Section to ARQUEVES. Weather was very fine, which included 6 sick animals, found standings somewhat dilapidated. Saw Town C. re poles for stables & corrugated iron	JHY
"	5-12-16		Usual section duties, raised roof of stable & started draining etc. Shot two horses one brought in by Motor Ambulance from AEUTHIEUL one with foot sloughing off.	
"	6-12-16		13 Horses were evacuated today. DDVS 5th Army called, another animal was shot near cookhouse	JHY
"	7-12-16		14 Animals admitted to Section. Received wire from D.R. stating that 50 animals were at ACHEUX STATION. with aid of some A.S.C men these were collected, and brought to Mobile Vet Section arriving 12-30 P.M. Unfortunately one animal got away on the road every endeavour was made to recover same without success.	JHY

Instructions regarding War Diaries and Intelligence Summaries are contained in F. S. Regs., Part II. and the Staff Manual respectively. Title pages will be prepared in manuscript.

WAR DIARY
or
INTELLIGENCE SUMMARY.
(Erase heading not required.)

28 MOBILE SECTION ARMY VETERINARY CORPS 37th Div

Army Form C. 2118.

Place	Date	Hour	Summary of Events and Information	Remarks and references to Appendices
ARQUEVES	8.12.16		Usual section duties erected cookhouse & pathways. Evacuated 18 animals from BELLE-EGLISE. ADVS called. Weather dull and cold. Distributed 59 remounts to various units. Sent search parties for lost remount, returned without any success. Reported to A.D.V.S.	JHY
"	9.12.16		Usual section duties, commenced to relay present horse standings.	JHY
"	10.12.16		3 animals admitted to section. Inspected men on parade. Capt Pryer arrived back from leave previous afternoon but took over A.D.V.S work, whilst Major Stephenson on leave. Went to see animal belonging to 3rd section D.A.C had been shot suffering from [illegible]	JHY
"	11.12.16		Inspected men on parade distributed clothing also gifts sent by Mrs Moore for A.V.C. N.C.O's. Then erected shelter for men. 8 animals admitted	JHY
"	12.12.16		15 animals admitted and 29 animals evacuated from BELLA EGLISE station. Motor ambulance brought in a case.	JHY
"	13.12.16		Received orders to prepare to move tomorrow 14.12.16. D.D.V.S. called and inspected place. 9 animals received and evacuated at BELLE EGLISE STATION. Ordered to be ready to move not later than 9 AM tomorrow. Weather fair	JHY
	14.12.16		Cleared camp, left two tents with T.M. and moved section off at 9-45 A.M for FOREN LE GRAND. arriving there at 5 P.M. Met by Capt Pryer who is acting as A.D.V.S + obtained good billets both for horses & men	JHY

A5834 Wt. W4973/M687 750,000 8/16 D. D. & L. Ltd. Forms/C.2118/13

Instructions regarding War Diaries and Intelligence Summaries are contained in F. S. Regs., Part II. and the Staff Manual respectively. Title Pages will be prepared in manuscript.

WAR DIARY
or
INTELLIGENCE SUMMARY
(Erase heading not required.)

Army Form C. 2118

Place	Date	Hour	Summary of Events and Information	Remarks and references to Appendices
FOHEN-LE GRAND	15·12·16		Section moved from here 9-30 A.M. destination FLERS. all animals fit. admitted one animal from Police, lame. Weather favourable but roads hilly arrived destination about 3 P.M.	DWY
FLERS.	16·12·16		Section move 9-30 AM. for MONCHIEL CAYEUX arrived at 2 P.M. good billet for men but horses in open weather favourable.	DWY
MONCHIEL CAYEUX	17·12·16		Section arrived here without any untoward incident at 3·30. Weather still favourable horses in the open but good billet for men.	DWY
NOYRENT FONTES	18·12·16		Section arrived at this stage at 3 PM after 5 hours march all the animals in good condition and no worse for the moving weather good. hard standings for horses in the open but sheltered. Men billeted in a school	DWY
ST. YENANT	19·12·16		Section arrived here about 2-30 horses and men little fatigued excellent standing for horses + good billet for men	DWY
"	20·12·16		One animal admitted to section sick. Went with Capt. Pryer to new area to look for suitable peace for section without result. Weather cold some snow.	DWY
"	21·12·16		Section duties resumed. Went with Capt. Pryer to Lestram for the purpose of find place for section found ~~farm~~ disused Barn at Fosse.	DWY
LESTRAM	22·12·16		Moved section to LESTRAM to temporary resting place Hard standing in open for horses men in barn	DWY
"	23·12·16		Usual section duties. went to HINGES. paid men. weather very unfavorable. Rain	DWY

1875 Wt. W593/826 1,000,000 4/15 J.B.C. & A. A.D.S.S./Forms/C. 2118.

Instructions regarding War Diaries and Intelligence Summaries are contained in F. S. Regs., Part II. and the Staff Manual respectively. Title Pages will be prepared in manuscript.

WAR DIARY
or
INTELLIGENCE SUMMARY
(Erase heading not required.)

Army Form C. 2118

37th Divn

Place	Date	Hour	Summary of Events and Information	Remarks and references to Appendices
LESTREM	24.12.16		Major J. R. STEEVENSON having returned from leave Capt. A. A. PRYER returned to section and resumed command. In morning with A.D.V.S. & D.A.A. & Q.M.G. 37th Div. to FOSSE to arrange for use of barn as stabling & also for billets for men. Think these will be available	A.A.P.
"	25.12.16		To FOSSE in morning to complete billeting arrangements. Decided to move next day. Gave NCO's & men Christmas dinner & the afternoon off. A quiet day.	A.A.P.
FOSSE	26.12.16		Moved section to FOSSE. Difficulty in getting infantry out of billet allotted to men of section.	A.A.P.
"	27.12.16		Spent day in arranging accommodation & preparing indents for material for stabling etc. Also checked mobilization equipment & prepared indents to complete refit after the operations on the ANCRE. Also prepared for evacuation next day.	A.A.P.
"	28.12.16		33 Animals evacuated from LA GORGUE.	A.A.P.
"	29.12.16		Under instructions from A.D.V.S. 37th Divn proceeded with 2 men to ANVIN & HEUCHIN to investigate cases of horses left behind by 126th Bde. R.F.A. on the recent march up. Halted for night at TANGRY. Heavy rain. Capt. J. H. YATES A.V.C. left in command of section	A.A.P.
"	30.12.16		To ANVIN & found the case left with DEPOT des CHEVAUX MALADES to be a case of gutter & a float case. Left it there accordingly. Found that the horse left at HEUCHIN had died. Proceeded back to FOSSE via FIEFS, LILLERS & ROBECQ. Prepared for evacuation next day.	A.A.P.
"	31.12.16		16 Animals evacuated from LA GORGUE. Ambulance made two journeys to railhead & then on to collect horse from C/123 R.F.A. at HAVERSKERQUE.	A.A.P.

A. A. Pryer. Capt. A.V.C.
O.C. 28th Mob. Vet. Section.

1875 Wt. W593/826 1,000,000 4/15 J.B.C. & A. A.D.S.S./Forms/C. 2118.

WAR DIARY

Vol 16

28th Mob Vet Sect

Jany 1917

28TH
MOBILE VETERINARY
SECTION.
No. Y 426
Date 1 - 2 - 17

To

34th Division "A"

Herewith War Diary for month of January 1917 please

[illegible]
Capt: AVC
O.C. 28th Mob: Vet: Section.

Instructions regarding War Diaries and Intelligence Summaries are contained in F. S. Regs., Part II. and the Staff Manual respectively. Title pages will be prepared in manuscript.

WAR DIARY
or
INTELLIGENCE SUMMARY.
(Erase heading not required.)

Army Form C. 2118.

Place	Date	Hour	Summary of Events and Information	Remarks and references to Appendices
FOSSE	1.1.17		Morning sick lines + office. Received orders from D.D.V.S. 1st Army to proceed to H.Q. D.V.S. forthwith for duty in office of D.V.S. Handed over imprest a/c + command of section to Capt. J.H. YATES A.V.C.	A.A.P.
"	2.1.17		Yesterday Capt. Pryer handed over section to me. also received various instructions from him, attended sick 26 horses were evacuated to base hospital.	JHY
"	3.1.17		Usual section duties 7 Horses + 3 mules were admitted to the section inspected cookhouse + saw the A.D.V.S. about material for stables.	JHY
"	4.1.17		15 Horses were admitted to mobile usual section duties started erecting hut for office Capt. Pryer left for D.V.S. office yesterday New Officer for division arrived and I took him round to his Brigade + handed over medicine chests etc to him.	JHY
"	5.1.17		13 Horses + 1 Mule admitted to Section and 29 horses + 5 mules evacuated. A.D.V.S. called cannot make a start on stables owing to no material arriving.	JHY
"	6.1.17		Usual section duties, morning at sick lines also 2 London H.B. + 1st Siege Anglesey R.E. [illegible] 2 Horses admitted	JHY
"	7.1.17		One mule + 3 horses admitted to section made a start on new stables material arriving very slow. 6 men from 9 North Staffords joined section for duty	JHY
	8.1.17		32 Horses + 1 Mule admitted to hospital also 8 men from D.A.C. ~~for~~ duty + discipline this the result of visit of G.O.C. on 5th inst. usual section	JHY
	9.1.17		43 horses and 2 mules were evacuated from section one mule admitted usual section duties went to St Venant + collected Horses left by D.A.C. + 126 Brigade R.F.A.	

A5834 Wt. W4973/M687 750,000 8/16 D. D. & L. Ltd. Forms/C.2118/13

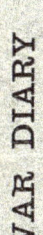

Instructions regarding War Diaries and Intelligence Summaries are contained in F. S. Regs., Part II. and the Staff Manual respectively. Title pages will be prepared in manuscript.

WAR DIARY
or
INTELLIGENCE SUMMARY.
(Erase heading not required.)

Army Form C. 2118.

23TH MOBILE VETERINARY SECTION.
No.........
Date.........

Place	Date	Hour	Summary of Events and Information	Remarks and references to Appendices
LA FOSSE	10.1.17		A.D.V.S. visited section, sold animal to butcher at LESTAIRS for 120 francs. Aeroplane (German) attacked balloon which is quite close to section, fortunately all horses were under cover. Attended sick + office	JHY
	11.1.17		Usual [illegible] section duties. [illegible] weather cold some snow	JHY
	12.1.17		27 Animals evacuated from section, [illegible] LA GARGUE station [illegible]	JHY
	13.1.17		Usual section duties 3 animals admitted to section, weather wet with some snow.	JHY
	14.1.17		3 animals admitted. all animals [illegible] brought in by M.T. [illegible] to stables. [illegible] section [illegible] separation [illegible]	JHY
	15.1.17		3 animals ~~were~~ affected with mange. [illegible] for A.D.V.S. ~~as~~ [illegible] C.R.E. re material for stables. Inspected saddles.	JHY
	16.1.17		Usual section routine, good progress made with stables. [illegible] Lance Sgt [illegible] was made paid acting Sergeant. 1 mule admitted [illegible]	
	17.1.17		Inspected [illegible] usual section duties. 1 horse admitted to section with mange	JHY
	18.1.17		2 horses admitted. [illegible] owing to order of A.D.V.S. [illegible] at base [illegible]	JHY
	19.1.17		Usual section duties. Inspected rifles. A.D.V.S. called [illegible] 2 horses 2 mules ~~[illegible]~~ admitted 4 Horses [illegible] all affected with mange.	JHY
	20.1.17		Inspected [illegible] 2 horses 2 mules admitted [illegible] weather very cold	JHY
	21.1.17		Usual section duties A.D.V.S. called 6 Animals admitted weather continues very cold.	JHY

A5834 Wt. W4973/M687 750,000 8/16 D. D. & L. Ltd. Forms/C.2118/13

Instructions regarding War Diaries and Intelligence Summaries are contained in F. S. Regs., Part II. and the Staff Manual respectively. Title pages will be prepared in manuscript.

WAR DIARY
or
INTELLIGENCE SUMMARY.
(Erase heading not required.)

28TH MOBILE VETERINARY SECTION.
No.......
Date.......

Army Form C. 2118.

Place	Date	Hour	Summary of Events and Information	Remarks and references to Appendices
LA FOSSE	22.1.17		Inspected rifles usual section duties 5 horses 4 mules admitted 3 evacuated 1 destroyed sold to French butcher as it was old & incurable severely cold	J.H.Y.
"	23.1.17		131 Animals arrived at LA GAUGRE Station Remounts assisted distribution of same Inspected harness, weather cold	J.H.Y.
"	24.1.17		A.D.V.S called Usual section duties G.O.C called 20 animals under treatment Weather conditions cold	J.H.Y.
"	25.1.17		Part of stables ready for occupation Col Humphreys called usual section duties inspected rifles also had 5 on parade. 14 loads of shale arrived	J.H.Y.
"	26.1.17		Usual section duties. 2 Remounts & 15 animals evacuated also 3 mange cases. 10 loads of shale arrived.	J.H.Y.
"	27.1.17		2 Horses & 1 Mule admitted to section. Usual section duties A.D.V.S called arranged with 2nd London H.B to shoe horses whilst shoeing smith on leave. Weather continues very cold 2 loads of brushwood & 2 loads of fascines arrived	J.H.Y.
"	28.1.17		Usual section duties, Inspected men and billets. 2 animals admitted to section weather very cold	J.H.Y.
"	29.1.17		Inspected men & harness. 3 or 4 interesting cases in section D.D.V.S called and expressed himself pleased with section A.D.V.S also called. Weather very cold	J.H.Y.
"	30.1.17		Section duties 2 animals with suspected mange admitted, Weather continues cold some snow fell Operated on two animals, A.D.V.S called	J.H.Y.
"	31.1.17		Stables completed, usual section duties two admissions to section Cold continues roads bad owing to coating of snow. 181 Animals admitted during month 160 Evacuated. 11 Cured	

Jno Hy Yates Capt AVC
O.C. 28 M.V.S

A5834 Wt. W4973/M687 750,000 8/16 D. D. & L. Ltd. Forms/C.2118/13

28TH
MOBILE VETERINARY
SECTION.
No. V 466
Date 1 - 3 - 17

To 37th Division "A"

Herewith War Diary for month of February, please.

Jno Hy Baker Capt: AVC
O.C. 28th Mobile Vety Section

Instructions regarding War Diaries and Intelligence Summaries are contained in F. S. Regs., Part II. and the Staff Manual respectively. Title Pages will be prepared in manuscript.

WAR DIARY
or
INTELLIGENCE SUMMARY
(Erase heading not required.)

Army Form C. 2118

Vol 17

Place	Date	Hour	Summary of Events and Information	Remarks and references to Appendices
LA FOSSE	1.2.17		Received orders to prepare to move. Interviewed O/C 1st London Mobile Veterinary Section & arranged with him to take over remaining cases. 10 animals admitted. A.D.V.S called	DHY
"	2.2.17		Sent 22 animals to 1/1 London Mobile Veterinary Section. Had float repaired. Sent pump to salvage. Weather continues very cold ice about 6 inches thick	DHY
"	3.2.17		Usual section duties. All prepared for move if necessary. A D V S called.	DHY
"	4.2.17		No admissions. Inspected men rifles etc. Usual section duties	DHY
"	5.2.17		Usual section duties. 4 animals several scrapings for mange with no result. Usual section duties	DHY
"	6.2.17		German aeroplanes (two) came over section about 1-20. Anti aircraft guns opened fire but no good results. Usual section duties. APM called.	DHY
"	7.2.17		More aeroplanes over section. Admitted 6 animals for treatment. A.D.V.S. called. Usual section duties. Weather continues very cold.	DHY
"	8.2.17		Received intimation that division moving to NOEUX LE MINES and section taking over from M.V.S of the 24 Division. Went over & saw O.C of mobile at DROUIN. Usual section duties. 6 animals admitted	DHY
"	9.2.17		6 animals admitted. Usual section duties. A.D.V.S called. Weather still very cold	DHY
"	10.2.17		Received instructions from A.D.V.S to move on 12 inst. Two men reported sick owing to severity of the weather. Had a mounted parade	
"	11.2.17		3 animals admitted. Usual section duties. 22 sick animals under treatment. Weather somewhat warmer frost breaking up.	
"	12.2.17		1 animal admitted. Usual section duties. A.D.V.S called. Sent S.S. & float to DOUVRIN where section will be situated. Weather continues warmer.	

1875 Wt. W593/826 1,000,000 4/15 J.B.C. & A. A.D.S.S./Forms/C. 2118.

Instructions regarding War Diaries and Intelligence Summaries are contained in F. S. Regs., Part II. and the Staff Manual respectively. Title pages will be prepared in manuscript.

WAR DIARY
or
INTELLIGENCE SUMMARY.
(Erase heading not required.)

23TH MOBILE VETERINARY SECTION. No. .... Date ....

Army Form C. 2118.

Place	Date	Hour	Summary of Events and Information	Remarks and references to Appendices
La Fosse	13.2.17	—	Moved section today to DROUVIN. 11 animals were evacuated to base. Left LA FOSSE 2 PM arrived DROUVIN 5-PM. New place well suited and fitted for a mobile section. Weather cold at nights	(initials)
DROUVIN	14.2.17	—	Started with section duties 9 animals admitted. A D V S called. Inspected 21 animals which arrived at NOEUX LES MINES station brought 3 remounts for 8th Lincolns to section. Weather very cold particularly nights	(initials)
"	15.2.17	—	Usual section duties 1 animal admitted went to see animal left at Paradis left behind by 37 DAC	(initials)
"	16.2.17		Sent float to Paradis for mule A D V S called 14 animals admitted to section float collected another case. Weather warmer + fine	(initials)
"	17.2.17		Weather continues warmer & fine usual section duties. 12 animals admitted to section with various diseases.	(initials)
"	18.2.17		1 animal admitted called on A D V S. usual section duties, weather continues warm but dull 47 animals under treatment	(initials)
"	19.2.17		Usual section duties inspected men on parade 10 animals admitted sick. A D V S called + selected 28 animals for evacuation. 2 cases of Stomatitis discovered	(initials)
"	20.2.17		Case of Tetanus died no evacuation on account of 2 more cases of Stomatitis being found amongst sick horses. Called to see A. D V S re these cases. 1 Horse died from colic that was affected with this disease	(initials)
"	21.2.17		13 animals admitted. 3 horses died, one from brain trouble 2 from eating Red Pierre Fosse. Carcases were sold to French butcher for 5 francs each.	(initials)
"	22.2.17		11 animals admitted. Usual section duties 5 men arrived from 39 [illegible] (1 for duty) A. D V S called	(initials)

A5834 Wt. W4973/M687 750,000 8/16 D. D. & L. Ltd. Forms/C.2118/13

Instructions regarding War Diaries and Intelligence Summaries are contained in F. S. Regs., Part II. and the Staff Manual respectively. Title Pages will be prepared in manuscript.

WAR DIARY
or
INTELLIGENCE SUMMARY
(Erase heading not required.)

Army Form C. 2118

23TH MOBILE VETERINARY SECTION. No........ Date........

Place	Date	Hour	Summary of Events and Information	Remarks and references to Appendices
DROUVIN	23·2·17		6 animals were admitted to the section and 43 evacuated to base. animals had to wait 4 hours at station for supply train which was late. weather fortunately fine.	JHY
"	24·2·17		Usual section duties. 11 animals admitted and one discharged cured. weather fine.	JHY
"	25·2·17		Usual section duties 1 animal admitted + 1 destroyed owing to breaking its back during the night. weather fine	JHY
"	26·2·17		10 animals admitted + 1 discharged cured, usual section duties. A.D.V.S. called weather fine	JHY
"	27·2·17		5 animals admitted 2 discharged cured 37 horses evacuated to base 2 discharged cured. Called to A.D.V.S. received orders for section to prepare to move.	JHY
"	28·2·17		Usual section duties. weather continues fine. 6 animals admitted. 1 discharged cured.	
			During the month 130 animals were admitted 113 " " Evacuated 13 " " Discharged cured 3 " died 3 " destroyed.	JHY
			The section was frequently visited by the A.D.V.S.	
			Jno Hy Yates Capt AVC O/c 28th M.V.S.	

1875 Wt. W593/826 1,000,000 4/15 J.B.C. & A. A.D.S.S./Forms/C. 2118.

MAR. 1917

WAR DIARY

Vol 18

28th Mob. VET. SECTION

28TH
MOBILE VETERINARY
SECTION.

No. V 79.6

Date 31 - 3 - 17.

To 37 Division A.

Herewith war diary for month ending March 31st 17.

[illegible] Capt AVC.
O/C 28th M.V.S

Instructions regarding War Diaries and Intelligence Summaries are contained in F. S. Regs., Part II. and the Staff Manual respectively. Title Pages will be prepared in manuscript.

WAR DIARY
or
INTELLIGENCE SUMMARY
(Erase heading not required.)

Army Form C. 2118

28TH MOBILE VETERINARY SECTION. No. .... Date ....

Place	Date	Hour	Summary of Events and Information	Remarks and references to Appendices
DROUVIN	1.3.17		One animal admitted to section A.D.V.S called & inspected animals for evacuation. Half of the section were medically examined for General Service. Weather cool but fine	JHY
"	2.3.17		13 animals evacuated to base one admitted sick usual section duties. All personal transport vehicles painted. 2 animals discharged cured.	JHY
"	3.3.17		O.C 33 M.V.S called & sent men to take over on animal discharged cured paid section & made preparations to move to NORRENT FONTES.	JHY
NORRENT.FONTES.	4.3.17		Left Drouvin 9-30 for NORRENT. FONTES. which place we arrive at 4-30. The weather was most favourable for the march being warm and sunny. and the roads in fairly good order 3 sick animals were left behind handed over to the incoming mobile (33. 6D).	JHY
" "	5.3.17		Usual section duties resumed weather colder animals in good condition the march down having little or no effect on them.	JHY
" "	6.3.17		A.D.V.S called at section. in the afternoon accompanied A.D.V.S to D.A.C. & other units.	
"	7.3.17		Weather continues cold, usual section duties. on account of the bitter cold wind had horses exercised 3 times. Went with A.D.V.S to 124 Brigade & 123 R.F.A.	JHY
"	8.3.17		Snow fell more or less all day & weather extremely cold. received orders for move tomorrow	JHY
ROCOURT	9.3.17		One animal admitted from 37 Div: Signals. Motor ambulance was telephoned for & took same to direct to Vety hospital. moved off for march to Rocourt at 9 AM prompt and arrived at that place 4-30. found a fairly good billet for Section.	JHY
"	10.3.17		Usual section duties resumed. nothing of importance occurred, weather fine	

1875 Wt. W593/826 1,000,000 4/15 J.B.C. & A. A.D.S.S./Forms/C. 2118.

Instructions regarding War Diaries and Intelligence Summaries are contained in F. S. Regs., Part II. and the Staff Manual respectively. Title Pages will be prepared in manuscript.

WAR DIARY
or
INTELLIGENCE SUMMARY
(Erase heading not required.)

28TH MOBILE VETERINARY SECTION.
No.
Date

Army Form C. 2118

Place	Date	Hour	Summary of Events and Information	Remarks and references to Appendices
ROCOURT	11-3-17		4 Animals admitted to Section held dress inspection. Received permission for leave from A.D.V.S. from 12-mid	
"	12-3-17		arranged with Capt Jewell to take over Section, & handed him imprest a/c. Took over command of section from Captain Yates, A.V.C. and received imprest a/c from him. Held rifle inspection and inspected all sick horses. Three animals were admitted to Section. A case of pneumonia died at 10 P.M.	H.J.
"	13-3-17		Performed usual duties in connection with Section. Fifteen animals were admitted to Section. Proceeded to 1st Cav. Pioneer Battalion and arranged for the sending in to Section of animal unfit to proceed on march. Saw A.D.V.S. & made arrangements with R.T.O. ST. POL to evacuate 3.30 P.M. 14-3-17.	H.J.
"	14-3-17		Performed usual duties in connection with Section. Admitted five animals. One animal died of pneumonia. Evacuated twenty-one animals & supervised loading at St. POL.	H.J.
"	15-3-17		Proceeded to ARMY TROOP SUPPLY COL. South of St. POL railway crossing and met 3rd Army Motor Horse ambulance (as arranged by A.D.V.S.) at 9.30 A.M. Proceeded in ambulance to PERNES and found the animal to be collected unable to rise so destroyed it. Proceeded thence to FAVX one mile SOUTH of PERNES to collect a mule & delivered it to 28 M.V.S. Admitted one case suspicious of Epizootic lymphangitis. Took smears and notified A.D.V.S. Six animals admitted to Section.	
"	16-3-17		Performed usual Section duties. Proceeded with horse ambulance to GAUCHIN VERLOINGT to collect an animal. Then proceeded to FLEURY on a similar errand and left ambulance at former place pending information as to state of case at FLEURY. Found it not necessary to use ambulance. Directed ambulance to return to Section & on the way bring in case from 37 D.A.C. Admitted 3 cases and destroyed one case suffering from debility & paraplegia.	H.J.

1875 Wt. W593/826 1,000,000 4/15 J.B.C. & A. A.D.S.S./Forms/C. 2118.

Instructions regarding War Diaries and Intelligence Summaries are contained in F. S. Regs., Part II. and the Staff Manual respectively. Title pages will be prepared in manuscript.

WAR DIARY
or
INTELLIGENCE SUMMARY.
(Erase heading not required.)

Army Form C. 2118.

23TH MOBILE VETERINARY SECTION.
No. ....
Date ....

Place	Date	Hour	Summary of Events and Information	Remarks and references to Appendices
ROCOURT	17-3-19		Proceeded to ARMY TROOP SUPPLY COL. and picked up Motor Horse Ambulance. Proceeded thence to ANVIN and collected horse left by 281st Bde. R.F.A. at depot for Clearing Malades. Returned with this horse to Section and admitted it. Paid out Section 595 francs having drawn 600 francs from 6th CORPS Cashier. Placed balance of 5 francs to imprest a/c. Deposited 25 francs (proceeds of sale of carcase of horse) with Field Cashier, 6th CORPS. Took sample of pus from suspicious abscess on inner side of thigh of mare belonging to A.D.C. 37th Division & forwarded to A.D.V.S.	H.J.
"	18-3-19		Proceeded to HERNICOURT to collect mule left by 416th (Edin) Field Coy, thence proceeded to HEUCHIN to collect a horse left by 21st D.A.C. Brought both these animals to Section. Carried out usual section duties. Two animals were admitted to Section.	H.J.
"	19-3-19		Admitted two animals from 126 H.B. brought in to Section by 3rd Army Motor Ambulance. Admitted a mule from 91st F. Coy. R.E. 15th Division. Performed usual Section duties.	H.J.
"	20-3-19		Proceeded in 3rd Army Motor Ambulance to MAZINGHEM N. OF ANVIN to collect H.D. left by 31 M.V.S. thence proceeded to SACHIN to collect another animal. Found this animal to have died and to have been buried on the premises of the Maire. Received a certificate to this effect. Brought one H.D. horse to Section in Motor Ambulance. Five animals in all were admitted to Section. Carried out usual Section duties. Arranged to evacuate 21 sick animals at 1.30 P.M. 21.3.19 from ST. POL.	H.J.

Instructions regarding War Diaries and Intelligence Summaries are contained in F. S. Regs., Part II. and the Staff Manual respectively. Title Pages will be prepared in manuscript.

WAR DIARY
or
INTELLIGENCE SUMMARY
(Erase heading not required.)

23rd MOBILE VETERINARY SECTION.
No.
Date

Army Form C. 2118

Place	Date	Hour	Summary of Events and Information	Remarks and references to Appendices
ROCOURT ST. LAURENT.	21·3·17		Performed usual section duties. Received from Divisional Sanitary Section three latrine boxes for use in Section. Arranged for provision of new latrine. Proceeded to ST. POL with 15 walking cases for evacuation (12 horses and 3 mules). Removed 6 horses for evacuation in 3rd Army Motor Ambulance. Superintended the loading of evacuation cases at ST. POL. Despatched two hides to the base (No: 22 Hospital).	
"	22·3·17		Performed usual Section duties. Made necessary preparations in the event of Section having to move. Received from B. Echelon 37 D.A.C. the hide of a horse belonging to No: 2 Section 4th D.A.C. which died in B. Echelon lines. Admitted one case to Section (mule from 152 Co. R.E.). Arranged to hold harness inspection 2 P.M. 23·3·17.	
"	23·3·17		Carried out usual Section duties. Admitted one case (P.U.R. 4th Middlesex). Held saddlery & harness inspection. Arranged to hold Rifle Inspection 9 A.M. 24·3·17. Captain Yates, A.V.C. returned to Section on leave from England. Handed over Section to him and Imprest Account. (five francs and seventy centimes).	
"	24·3·17		~~Returned~~ Section handed over by Cpl. Sewell found everything correct three ~~one~~ animal sick A.D.V.S called	
"	25·3·17		Inspected men. Called at 4 division mobile & saw O/C & A.D.V.S ~~&~~ Div arranged with him to take over sick at Monchy Bretton. & sent two.	
	26·3·17		4 animals admitted went to D.A.C also went to Haute Coté & fetched animal from inhabitant, one also fetched from AUVIN. & PERNES.	

1875 Wt. W593/826 1,000,000 4/15 J.B.C. & A. A.D.S.S./Forms/C. 2118.

Army Form C. 2118

Instructions regarding War Diaries and Intelligence Summaries are contained in F. S. Regs., Part II. and the Staff Manual respectively. Title Pages will be prepared in manuscript.

WAR DIARY
or
INTELLIGENCE SUMMARY
(Erase heading not required.)

23rd MOBILE VETERINARY SECTION.
No.
Date.

Place	Date	Hour	Summary of Events and Information	Remarks and references to Appendices
ROCOURT	27.3.17.		Fetched horses from Caumont, Bingal, + Pernes with motor ambulance A.D.V.S called Two cases of stomatitis from 17 Division	
"	28.3.17		Evacuated 12 animals and collected 2 animals from Autromichy also found that 3 others had been left behind by same unit. visited the D.A.C.	
"	29.3.17		Collected with Motor ~~Horse~~ Ambulance 2 animals from Marie of Automeley saw D.D.V.S.	
"	30.3.17		Visited D.A.C with Capt. Sewell re sam horses. A.D.V.S called 4 animals admitted to section collected 1 Ho: at HEUCHIN + 1 Ho at ~~[illegible]~~ TEIFS. with Motor Horse Ambulance	
"	31.3.17		Collected 1 Ho at ANVIN + 1 at Saulicourt. with M.H.A. also two animals from REBRUVIETTE and destroyed one being ~~[illegible]~~ too weak to move. to Section.	
			29 Animals have been collected by this Section whilst stationed here. All these were float cases. The Section has been frequently visited by A.D.V.S.	
			70 animals have be evacuated during the month.	
			[signature] Capt. A.V.C. O/c 28th MVS	

1875 Wt. W593/826 1,000,000 4/15 J.B.C. & A. A.D.S.S./Forms/C. 2118.

Subject: War Diaries

37th Divn 901

SECRET

D A G
Base

Herewith War Diary of 28th Mobile Vet. Section for April 1917.

S. Dunscombe Capt.
for Major General
Commanding 37th Division

25/5/17

Instructions regarding War Diaries and Intelligence Summaries are contained in F. S. Regs., Part II. and the Staff Manual respectively. Title Pages will be prepared in manuscript.

WAR DIARY
or
INTELLIGENCE SUMMARY
(Erase heading not required.)

Army Form C. 2118

37

Mob Vety Sec

Vol 19

Place	Date	Hour	Summary of Events and Information	Remarks and references to Appendices
ROCOURT ST LAURENT	1·4·17		Section duties. Went with Motor Horse Ambulance to HERNICOURT, and collected heavy draught horse left behind by departing unit. collected 1 animal from ST MICHEL. ADVS called	
	2·4·17		Usual section duties [illegible] Motor Horse Ambulance and collected 4 animals from [illegible] of HOUCHIN left by [illegible] units, [illegible] to ADVS. 4 other animals [illegible] left with [illegible]. Weather cold [illegible] night snowing [illegible]	
	3·4·17		Usual section duties, brought in [illegible] from FILLIEVRES. with Motor Ambulance. ADVS called and [illegible] instructions [illegible] to move to DUISANS. with section [illegible] 6 animals admitted to section. [illegible] destroyed	
"	4·4·17		29 animals evacuated ADVS reported sick [illegible] D.D.V.S. [illegible] duties for [illegible] [illegible] instruction to move to DUISANS.	
DUISANS	5·4·17		[illegible] left ROCOURT 7.30. & arrived DUISANS [illegible] P.M. [illegible] and billets for men. Weather conditions splendid	
	6·4·17		Called at ADVS Office and [illegible] section duties [illegible] all day [illegible] shelled	
"	7·4·17		Called at ADVS Office [illegible] also [illegible] and selected [illegible] for [illegible] advanced section [illegible] left [illegible] the road [illegible]	
	8·4·17		[illegible]	
			[illegible] at ADVS [illegible]	
	9·4·17		[illegible] section duties, [illegible] animals [illegible]	
	10·4·17		[illegible] with ADVS [illegible]	
	11·4·17		10 animals [illegible] many [illegible] Sir Douglas Haigh	

1875 Wt. W593/826 1,000,000 4/15 J.B.C. & A. A.D.S.S./Forms/C. 2118.

Army Form C. 2118

Instructions regarding War Diaries and Intelligence Summaries are contained in F. S. Regs., Part II. and the Staff Manual respectively. Title Pages will be prepared in manuscript.

WAR DIARY
or
INTELLIGENCE SUMMARY
(Erase heading not required.)

Place	Date	Hour	Summary of Events and Information	Remarks and references to Appendices
DUISANS.	12.4.17		Usual section duties [illegible] mobile [illegible] animals [illegible]	
	13.4.17		[illegible] animals admitted [illegible] [illegible] called. received orders to prepare to move.	
LIGNEREUIL	14.4.17		25 Horses & mules evacuated from Agny. Section moved to LIGNEREUIL arriving 6-30 P.M.	
LIGNEREUIL	15.4.17		animals in the open. weather fine but cold. Section duties.	
"	16.4.17		Usual section duties, went over to AMBRINES & inspected [illegible] cavalry. weather wet.	
	17.4.17		Usual section duties. Rode to TINQUES to [illegible] 8 animals admitted	
"	18.4.17		[illegible] 2 cavalry horses from AMBRINES. 1 evacuated [illegible] weather very wet.	
"	19.4.17		Usual section duties. A.D.V.S. called. animals admitted.	
"	20.4.17		Received orders to [illegible] A.V.C. Sgt. [illegible]	
ETURN	21.4.17		Section moved to ETURN. [illegible] G.O.C. [illegible] took over 14 animals [illegible] 4 M.V.S.	
"	22.4.17		Usual section duties. Went with A.D.V.S. [illegible] 10 animals admitted [illegible]	
"	23.4.17		Usual section duties & animals admitted [illegible]	

1875 Wt. W593/826 1,000,000 4/15 J.B.C. & A. A.D.S.S./Forms/C. 2118.

Army Form C. 2118.

Instructions regarding War Diaries and Intelligence Summaries are contained in F. S. Regs., Part II, and the Staff Manual respectively. Title pages will be prepared in manuscript.

WAR DIARY
or
INTELLIGENCE SUMMARY.

(Erase heading not required.)

Place	Date	Hour	Summary of Events and Information	Remarks and references to Appendices
ETUAN	24.4.17		Evacuated 26 animals from [illegible]. 1 animal died from [illegible] [illegible] very fine	
"	25.4.17		27 animals admitted to section. [illegible] [illegible] under repair	
"	26.4.17		32 animals evacuated [illegible]	
"	27 [illegible]		[illegible]	
	28.4.17		[illegible]	
	29 [illegible]		Received orders to move [illegible]	

28 MOBILE SECTION - ARMY VETERINARY CORPS.
1-6-17

To 37. Division

A.

Herewith war diary
for month ending 31-5-17

[illegible] Capt AVC
O.C. 28th M.V.S

Instructions regarding War Diaries and Intelligence Summaries are contained in F. S. Regs., Part II. and the Staff Manual respectively. Title Pages will be prepared in manuscript.

WAR DIARY
or
INTELLIGENCE SUMMARY
(Erase heading not required.)

Army Form C. 2118

-28 MOBILE SECTION- ARMY VETERINARY CORPS.

Vol 20

Place	Date	Hour	Summary of Events and Information	Remarks and references to Appendices
LIGNEREUIL	1.5.17		Moved section on this date from ETRUN. weather favourable. sent for animal found by A.D.V.S at GIVENCHY-LE-NOBLE	
"	2.5.17		Sent float to ETURN for remainder of stores and animal left behind usual section duties weather fine	
"	3.5.17		Took veterinary charge of Canadian Forestry. 47 Reserve Park & 48 Field Ambulance visited same A.D.V.S called weather fine	
"	4.5.17		Usual section duties improved lines & forge attended sick and visited units.	
"	5.5.17		8 Animals admitted to section since 1st inst all under treatment weather fine	
"	6.5.17		Usual section duties A.D.V.S called	
"	7.5.17		1 Animal admitted started painting transports weather continues fine	
"	8.5.17		A.D.V.S called 1 animal admitted	
"	9.5.17		Usual section duties	
"	10.5.17		9 Animals sent to base called on units	
"	11.6.17		Usual section duties A.D.V.S called inspected Harness & saddlery	
"	12.6.17		Weather fine usual section duties inspected rifles	
"	13.6.17		Show of chargers of division A.D.V.S called. inspected men	

1875 Wt. W593/826 1,000,000 4/15 J.B.C. & A. A.D.S.S./Forms/C. 2118.

Instructions regarding War Diaries and Intelligence Summaries are contained in F. S. Regs., Part II. and the Staff Manual respectively. Title Pages will be prepared in manuscript.

WAR DIARY
or
INTELLIGENCE SUMMARY
(Erase heading not required.)

Army Form C. 2118

-28 MOBILE SECTION- ARMY VETERINARY CORPS

Place	Date	Hour	Summary of Events and Information	Remarks and references to Appendices
LIGNEREUIL	14.5.17		Visited units Capt Sewell being on leave took over his charges etc	
"	15.5.17		Usual section duties 2 animals admitted weather colder. Had an inter-section competition for cleanest horses & men	
	16.5.17		Went with ADVS to units and LA CAUROY. 1 animal admitted usual duties weather dull & rain at night	
"	17.5.17		Received instructions to prepare to move sent mule (Signals) to 27 M.V.S. usual section duties	
~~Walu~~ WARLUS	18.5.17		Moved from LIGNEREUIL to WARLUS. weather fine left 3 animals in charge of 11. M.V.S. 3rd Div	
"	19.5.17		Section duties A.D.V.S inspected sick, weather fine	
"	20.5.17		Usual section duties, went with A.D.V.S to Porte de ARMIENS & inspected new place	
ARRAS.	21.5.17		arrived here this date about 10 A.M. took over from 1st/1st London Mobile 56 Division the late O.C of that unit had been killed by a bomb a few days previous took over 2 animals many others were admitted to Section	
"	22.5.17		Usual section duties about 20 animals admitted weather ~~[illegible]~~ hot. at night enemy sent over a few shells.	
"	23.5.17		Evacuated 32 Animals including 12 mange cases A.D.V.S called heavy shelling towards 12 P.M at night	
"	24.5.17		A.D.V.S Called 20 animals admitted from Heavy Batty & 35th with Mange shelling at night	

1875 Wt. W593/826 1,000,000 4/15 J.B.C. & A. A.D.S.S./Forms/C. 2118.

Instructions regarding War Diaries and Intelligence Summaries are contained in F. S. Regs., Part II. and the Staff Manual respectively. Title Pages will be prepared in manuscript.

WAR DIARY
or
INTELLIGENCE SUMMARY
(Erase heading not required.)

Army Form C. 2118

28 MOBILE SECTION ARMY VETERINARY CORPS

Place	Date	Hour	Summary of Events and Information	Remarks and references to Appendices
ARRAS.	25.5.17.		Enemy sent 4 or 5 heavy shells over early this morning. some falling near the Section ADVS Called 25 animals admitted to section a great majority were affected with contagious diseases. A mare foaled in section. a healthy colt foal. Enemy aeroplanes over section in early hours of the morning. 8 wounded mules sent in from 15 O R E.	
"	26.5.17		Evacuated 45 horses 75 mules to Base Hospital 1 admitted called at ADVS office usual section duties.	
"	27.5.17		Weather continues fine only one shell came over this morning usual section duties ADVS called. Visited attached units	
"	28.5.17		Usual section duties. ADVS called, one animal (unit RGA) strayed from lines turned Section out to find same	
"	29.5.17		Operated on 4 Shrapnel cases. ~~Ⓔ~~ Two Tetanus cases recovering usual Section duties called on units 9 animals admitted	
"	30.5.17		16 Animals evacuated to Base. Sgt Moyes left Section. being a T.E. man. This Sgt has done good work whilst in France & his loss is regretted	
"	31.5.17		Weather continued fine usual. section duties. During the month the Section has been frequently visited by the ADVS. Many cases belonging to outside units have been treated during this last fortnight & cured. The immediate vicinity of the Section has been shelled. & the O.C ~~[illegible]~~ of section previously situated here. was killed by aerial bombs.	[illegible] Capt AVC OC 28th M.V.S

1875 Wt. W593/826 1,000,000 4/15 J.B.C. & A. A.D.S.S./Forms/C. 2118.

War Diary

SECRET

No 21

Dr Mobile Section

June 1917

Army Form C. 2118

Instructions regarding War Diaries and Intelligence Summaries are contained in F. S. Regs., Part II. and the Staff Manual respectively. Title Pages will be prepared in manuscript.

WAR DIARY
or
INTELLIGENCE SUMMARY
(Erase heading not required.)

Place	Date	Hour	Summary of Events and Information	Remarks and references to Appendices
ARRAS.	1.6.17		Usual section duties A.D.V.S called received orders to prepare to move weather fine	
"	2.6.17		Sent section forward to LIGNEREUIL at 8-45 A.M remained behind with sick 5 which I evacuated from ARRAS Station eight or ten shells were sent over the town before I left. arrived at LIGNEREUIL about 6 P.M.	
LIGNEREUIL	3.6.17		Usual section duties weather fine. Sick animals making satisfactory progress	
"	4.6.17		A.D.V.S called 2 animals admitted usual section duties	
"	5.6.17		Usual section duties. Held rifle inspection & Box respirators weather very hot	
"	6.6.17		went to St Pol inspected kits, animal admitted from 50th Field ambulance yesterday	
VALHOUN	7.6.17		Left LIGNEREUIL at 6-45 A.M. with section, instructed to proceed to VALHOUN arrived at the latter place soon after ~~noon~~ 12 P.M. weather fine. visited Signals 40th Co & other units, no mishaps or accidents en route	
"	8.6.17		Left VALHOUN at 5-45 with section to proceed to LUGY arriving there at 12.45 P.M. weather warm and we proceeded by easy stages found an excellent site for Mobile which had been selected by the A.D.V.S.	

1875 Wt. W593/826 1,000,000 4/15 J.B.C. & A. A.D.S.S./Forms/C. 2118.

Instructions regarding War Diaries and Intelligence Summaries are contained in F. S. Regs., Part II. and the Staff Manual respectively. Title Pages will be prepared in manuscript.

WAR DIARY
or
INTELLIGENCE SUMMARY
(Erase heading not required.)

Army Form C. 2118

Place	Date	Hour	Summary of Events and Information	Remarks and references to Appendices
LUCY	9.6.17		Usual section duties, none of the animals looked any worse for their long trek. Operated on big bay geld: A.D.V.S called. Visited No 2 Co. Train	
"	10.6.17		Men in excellent spirits and Section horses very fit. Yesterday sent for Sgt Parsons who had instructions to proceed here in place of Sgt Moyes	
"	11.6.17		Inspected rifles. had all transport washed and inspected weather continues fine. visited No 62 Train	
"	12.6.17		Section duties improved cookhouse and also lines, rained during night	
"	13.6.17		Usual section duties inspected Harness and saddlery operated on 2 horses weather continues fine	
"	14.6.17		A.D.V.S called. usual section duties. Went to Svin re evacuations. no conveyance. A.D.M.S called.	
"	15.6.17		Inspected rifles Office work usual section duties. A.D.M.S called weather continues very fine	
"	16.6.17		Usual duties. called at HQ at Bomy. 1 animal admitted.	
"	17.6.17		Started at 3 AM with Sgt & 4 men for Veterinary Hospital at St OMER arrived at 12 P.M. This is the first time animals have been evacuated by road from Section. arrived back at Section 8 P.M. distance covered about 40 miles	

1875 Wt. W593/826 1,000,000 4/15 J.B.C. & A. A.D.S.S./Forms/C. 2118.

Instructions regarding War Diaries and Intelligence Summaries are contained in F. S. Regs., Part II. and the Staff Manual respectively. Title pages will be prepared in manuscript.

WAR DIARY
or
INTELLIGENCE SUMMARY.
(Erase heading not required.)

Army Form C. 2118.

61

Place	Date	Hour	Summary of Events and Information	Remarks and references to Appendices
LUGY	18.6.17		2 Horses + 1 Mule admitted to section made arrangements for swimming place for men. Had mounted drill. weather fine	
"	19.6.17		Usual section duties saddlery inspection, animal admitted. Weather fine	
"	20.6.17		6 Horses + 1 mule evacuated by road to St Omer in charge of Sgt. usual section duties. Some showers during day.	
"	21.6.17		2 animals admitted sent 2 more by road to St Omer. weather showery	
"	22.6.17		Wired for Motor Ambulance + evacuated 2 Horses usual section duties received orders to move. Weather very wet	
"	23.6.17		Section Moved at 6-45 from here. weather improved. Found at ESTREE-BLANCHE animal belonging to NRR practically unable to move ~~and same~~ placed with an inhabitant. arrived at destination STEENBEQUE. 2-30.	
STEENBECQUE	24.6.17		Section moved 4-45 for starting point arrived punctually and marched forward to our destination LOCRE. no incident of note occurred Men + horses finished the long journey splendidly. Men accommodated in Tents horses in the open. saw the GOC re/animal left behind weather good.	
LOCRE	25.6.17		Took over duties of A/ADVS Rs Capt Heston. Inspected various units attached to HQ	

A5834 Wt. W4973/M687 750,000 8/16 D. D. & L. Ltd. Forms/C.2118/13.

Instructions regarding War Diaries and Intelligence Summaries are contained in F. S. Regs., Part II. and the Staff Manual respectively. Title Pages will be prepared in manuscript.

WAR DIARY
or
INTELLIGENCE SUMMARY
(Erase heading not required.)

Army Form C. 2118

Place	Date	Hour	Summary of Events and Information	Remarks and references to Appendices
LOCRE	26.6.17.		Usual section duties. Visited all H Q units. Attended 49 Field Ambulance. Aerial Bombs were dropped on this unit causing 9 animals deaths and 6 wounded	JHY
"	27.6.17		Visited 49th Field Ambulance & destroyed mule 3 were admitted to Section with various wounds. 2 other mules from other units.	JHY
"	28.6.17		~~[illegible]~~. Visited units 6 Horses admitted, weather fine. Signed returns etc for D.D.V.S.	JHY
"	29.6.17		Visited Units, usual section duties & etc. Visited Corps Dep. also Corps Veterinary Dept.	JHY
"	30.6.17		H Q moved A.D.V.S returned. 1 animal died 1 destroyed 49th Field ambulance 8 Horses & 3 Mules admitted 1 Horse handed to 48th M.V.S.	
			During the month 34 Horses, 15 Mules, 49 Total were admitted to Section. 24 were evacuated to Base. 10 animals were returned to units cured. 2 Destroyed 2 Died.	JHY
			A.D.V.S. frequently visited Section.	

Jno. Hy. Yates Capt. AVC
O.C. 28th M.V.S.

1875 Wt. W593/826 1,000,000 4/15 J.B.C. & A. A.D.S.S./Forms/C. 2118.

Vol 22

War Diary

28th Mob Vet Section

JULY 1917

37th Division

"Q."

Herewith Diary (War) for Month of July 1917

J.W.H. Wale

Capt A.V.C.

O.C. 38th Mobile Vety Section

1/8/17.

Instructions regarding War Diaries and Intelligence Summaries are contained in F. S. Regs., Part II. and the Staff Manual respectively. Title Pages will be prepared in manuscript.

WAR DIARY
or
INTELLIGENCE SUMMARY
(Erase heading not required.)

Army Form C. 2118

Place	Date	Hour	Summary of Events and Information	Remarks and references to Appendices
LOCRE	1/7/17	—	D.A.D.V.S Called, Inspected Sick. Accompanied D.A.D.V.S to B Achelon D.A.C + inspected their animals. also took Vety charge of this unit. 9 Sick admitted to section.	[illegible]
"	2.7.17		Usual Section duties 26 animals admitted to Section. Called to see a Butcher about purchasing of useless animals at BAILLEUIL.	[illegible]
"	3.7.17		Corps A.D.V.S called also Col. Elwiss + inspected section. D.A.D.V.S called later + inspected ~~sick~~ sick for evacuation. B Achelon of 37 D.A.C had 2 Mules accidentally injured by a bomb. weather cloudy but fine. 12 animals admitted	[illegible]
"	4.7.17		35 animals evacuated by road to St OMER today 4 animals admitted including A.D.V.S of Corps called. Sold animal to Butcher for 150 Francs.	
"	5.7.17		Admitted 4 animals to section. visited D.A.C received orders to move to DANOUTRE	
"	6.7.17		D.A.D.V.S called section duties + be moved to DANOUTRE. Evacuated 10 foal-cases to Corps Mobile Veterinary Detch admitted 6 cases one of which was transferred to 31st MVS	
DRANOUTRE	7.7.17		10 tents + 1 armstrong hut pump and watertrough handed over to 31st M.V.S. 1 admitted to section usual section duties ordered material for erection of cookhouse forage barn etc. also sand for improvement of standings.	
"	8.7.17.		Usual section duties 9 animals admitted rain during night.	

Instructions regarding War Diaries and Intelligence Summaries are contained in F. S. Regs., Part II. and the Staff Manual respectively. Title Pages will be prepared in manuscript.

WAR DIARY
or
INTELLIGENCE SUMMARY
(Erase heading not required.)

Army Form C. 2118

Place	Date	Hour	Summary of Events and Information	Remarks and references to Appendices
DRANOUTRE	9-7-17		Visited D.A.C usual section duties Corps A.D.V.S called. 10 Men attached for duty 10 casualties admitted DADVS called. handed over yesterday to 49 Field Ambulance 4 Riders. they having become surplus.	
"	10.7.17		Usual section duties 5 casualties admitted. DADVS called Driver Donaldson was kicked whilst doing stable guard. & taken to 50 Field Ambulance.	
"	11.7.17		Sold 2 Horses to butcher for 50 & 200 francs. Evacuated to St OMER 35 animals. 7 admitted. DADVS called. General Potts visited section	
"	12.7.17		Usual section duties. 5 animals admitted Started building shed re the Paid section Artillery joins division. 2 Animals sent to Units cured	
"	13.7.17		2 Casualties admitted. Visited D.A.C. also DADVS took over charge of whole of D.A.C also C Batty 124.	
"	14.7.17		Usual section duties visited units. took charge Veterinary of D.A.C & other units 3 animals admitted.	
"	15.7.17		D.A.D.V.S called also Corps A.D.V.S. [illegible] Staff Sergeant arrived from base this is an addition to section weather continues fine	
"	16.7.17		8 Casualties admitted 3 animals discharged cured to units	

1875 Wt. W593/826 1,000,000 4/15 J.B.C. & A. A.D.S.S./Forms/C. 2118.

Instructions regarding War Diaries and Intelligence Summaries are contained in F. S. Regs., Part II. and the Staff Manual respectively. Title Pages will be prepared in manuscript.

WAR DIARY
or
INTELLIGENCE SUMMARY
(Erase heading not required.)

Army Form C. 2118

Place	Date	Hour	Summary of Events and Information	Remarks and references to Appendices
DRANOUTRE	17.7.17.		One animal admitted 1 discharged cured 1 sold to Butcher. usual section duties ~~Section mounted and ...~~	
"	18.7.17		Evacuated 13 Horses, 1 admitted 2 discharged cured. visited DAC & other units DADVS called	
"	19.7.17		Usual section duties built new cook house 3 casualties admitted DADVS called ~~visited units~~	
"	20.7.17		4 Animals admitted 1 discharged cured Weather continues fine DADVS called	
"	21.7.17		Visited units, Mange case admitted & scrapings examined cured, sent to unit DADVS called. Painted lumber & signs etc.	
"	22.7.17		Usual section duties admitted 4 casualties DADVS called.	
"	23.7.17		Visited all units, also usual section duties. 2 patients discharged cured 6 admitted	
"	24.7.17		7 Casualties admitted. Animal sent to Butcher. 1 cured to unit	
"	25.7.17		Usual section duties 7 animals admitted evacuated 19 Horses 3 mules to base Hospital 4 cured to unit	
"	26.7.17		2 Animals admitted visited units inspected rifles	

Instructions regarding War Diaries and Intelligence Summaries are contained in F. S. Regs., Part II. and the Staff Manual respectively. Title Pages will be prepared in manuscript.

WAR DIARY
or
INTELLIGENCE SUMMARY
(Erase heading not required.)

Army Form C. 2118

Place	Date	Hour	Summary of Events and Information	Remarks and references to Appendices
DRANOUTRE	27.7	17	Usual section duties 5 Casualties admitted. Inspected harness visits units. Visits Corps dips from 7 AM to 10 AM	
"	28.7	17	DADVS called improved buildings & standings visited units.	
"	29.7	17	1 Animal admitted 1 cured & DADVS called usual section duties. rain most of the day	
"	30.7	17	5 Casualties admitted 2 cured & sent to unit. weather dull & damp	
"	31.7	17	Rifle inspection. ADVS of Corps called. Visited Batteries with DADVS. also units Inspected mens kits &c.	
			During the month. The Section was visited by the Corps A.D.V.S. Daily by the DADVS. 87 Horses & 16 Mules were evacuated to Base Hospital by road. Improvements were made to Standings new cook house built. also Office & Pharmacy. 4 Cases of Mange were treated Successfully. 32 Cases. cured and returned to various units this is a record for section 5 animals were sold to Butchers for food	

Geo Hy Yale Capt AVC O.C. 28th M.V.S.

1875 Wt. W593/826 1,000,000 4/15 J.B.C. & A. A.D.S.S./Forms/C. 2118.

VR 23

Hardinay

28 Mot Vet Sec

Aug 1917

Instructions regarding War Diaries and Intelligence Summaries are contained in F. S. Regs., Part II. and the Staff Manual respectively. Title pages will be prepared in manuscript.

WAR DIARY
or
INTELLIGENCE SUMMARY.
(Erase heading not required.)

Army Form C. 2118.

Place	Date	Hour	Summary of Events and Information	Remarks and references to Appendices
DRANOUTRE				
"	1.8.17		Usual section duties 3 Animals admitted. 22 animals evacuated.	[illegible]
"	2.8.17		Inspected Rifles & Equipment section duties	
"	3.8.17		2 Animal admitted Visited units section duties	[illegible]
"	4.8.17		3 — do — D.A.D.V.S called 1 Animal returned to unit cured	
"	5.8.17		Usual section duties 8 casualties admitted 3 returned to units cured	[illegible]
"	6.8.17		11 animals admitted inspected harness etc 1 animal cured to unit	
"	7.8.17		11 — do — do 2 animals cured usual section duties	[illegible]
"	8.8.17		5 — do do Evacuated 30 to Base. Section moved to LOCRE	
LOCRE	9.8.17		8 animals left by 31st Mobile usual section duties 5 cases admitted	[illegible]
"	10.8.17		Usual section duties visited DAC + other units. 6 casualties admitted	
"	11.8.17		Inspected rifles + harness DADVS called 4 animals admitted visited units 1 animal destroyed + 1 issued to division	[illegible]
"	12.8.17		5 animals admitted. usual section duties improved stables and built new cookhouse	
"	13.8.17		9 casualties admitted visited all units inspected harness & vehicles, 2 animals destroyed 1 died	[illegible]
"	14.8.17		10 Casualties admitted DADVS called usual section duties 2 cured to units	

A5834 Wt. W4973/M687 750,000 8/16 D. D. & L. Ltd. Forms/C.2118/13

Instructions regarding War Diaries and Intelligence Summaries are contained in F. S. Regs., Part II. and the Staff Manual respectively. Title Pages will be prepared in manuscript.

WAR DIARY
or
INTELLIGENCE SUMMARY
(Erase heading not required.)

-28 MOBILE SECTION- ARMY VETERINARY CORPS.

Army Form C. 2118

Place	Date	Hour	Summary of Events and Information	Remarks and references to Appendices
LOCRE.	15.8.17.		Inspected equipment. usual section duties 7 casualties admitted 2 cured to units 41 animals evacuated to base	JM
"	16.8.17		DADVS called usual section work visited units 1 admitted	
"	17.8.17		Visited units. 1 admitted. drained camp during the week and made several improvements. Bombs ~~were~~ seen to drop near section	JM
"	18.8.17		Visited 152 R.E. bomb had dropped on horse line killing 16 & wounded 9 which were admitted to section.	JM
"	19.8.17		Visited units Men paraded to Church. weather fine. 1 animal admitted	JM
"	20.8.17		Inspected Men's Kits 10 casualties admitted weather fine A.D.V.S called	
"	21.8.17		6 animals admitted inspected harness & saddlery etc D.A.D.V.S called	JM
"	22.8.17		Inspected Rifles 23 animals evacuated by road. 6 cases of suspected stomatitis. 3 casualties. D A D V S called.	
"	23.7.17		Usual section duties 7 animals admitted weather still fine visited units	JM
"	24.7.17		Weather somewhat colder usual section duties no admissions DADVS called	JM
"	25.7.17		Usual section duties weather conditions showery 5 animals admitted	
"	26.7.17		Weather wet. Gave section few hours off in afternoon DADVS called	

1875 Wt. W593/826 1,000,000 4/15 J.B.C. & A. A.D.S.S./Forms/C. 2118.

Instructions regarding War Diaries and Intelligence Summaries are contained in F. S. Regs., Par. II, and the Staff Manual respectively. Title pages will be prepared in manuscript.

WAR DIARY
or
INTELLIGENCE SUMMARY.
(Erase heading not required.)

28 MOBILE SECTION – ARMY VETERINARY CORPS.

Army Form C. 2118.

Place	Date	Hour	Summary of Events and Information	Remarks and references to Appendices
LOCRE	27·8·17		Usual section duties DADVS. called inspected Rifles visited units	[illegible]
"	28·8·17		4 casualties admitted. inspected Harness visited ASC Companies	[illegible]
"	29·8·17		6 animals discharged (5 cured) weather very unfavourable ADVS (Corps) inspected unit. visited ASC & other units	[illegible]
"	30·8·17		9 animals admitted. Visited units usual section duties. 2 Discharged cured	[illegible]
"	31·8·17		4 animals —do—.	
			During the month 39 animals were discharged to various units cured. as against 45 previous month The latter being a record as far as this unit is concerned 109 animals were evacuated. 6 animals were destroyed for various reasons 3 of them being sold to butcher for food. and 5 animals died. During the month the stables were concreated. Cook house built drainage of camp improved and many other improvements were made. The section was visited daily by DADVS. and 5 times by ADVS Corps	[illegible]
			Tolty Yates Capt } 31·8·17 O.C. 28th M.V.S.	

A6945 Wt. W11422/M1160 350,000 12/16 D. D. & L. Forms/C./2118/14.

War Diary

28 Mob Vet Section

Sept 1917

Vol 24

28TH
MOBILE VETERINARY
SECTION.

No. ......

Date 3/10/17

To/ 37 Division 'A'.

Herewith War Diary
for month ending
Sept. 30th 1917.

[illegible] Capt.

O.C. 28th M.V.S.

Instructions regarding War Diaries and Intelligence Summaries are contained in F. S. Regs., Part II. and the Staff Manual respectively. Title pages will be prepared in manuscript.

WAR DIARY
or
INTELLIGENCE SUMMARY.
(Erase heading not required.)

28TH MOBILE VETERINARY SECTION.
No. ....
Date. ....

Army Form C. 2118.

Place	Date	Hour	Summary of Events and Information	Remarks and references to Appendices
LOCRE	1/9/17		Inspected rifles. Usual section duties. 3 animals admitted to section	[initials]
"	2/9/17		Admissions to Section 5. All cases of shell wounds by E.A. 35 animals were evacuated by Rail entrained at HAGENDOORNE. One animal was destroyed in Section for a fractured leg.	[initials]
"	3.9.17		During night E.A. were busy. Two machines coming down to within 200 ft. of Section. Bombing continued at intervals throughout the night. A.D.V.S (Corps) visited Section. Handed charge of section to Capt. Huston having been granted leave for 10 days.	[initials]
"	4.9.17		Took over charge of section from Capt Yates. Capt Yates being granted ten days leave. Admission to section 3 animals. Discharged cured to duty 4.	W.H.
	5.9.17		Admission 10 animals to section evacuated to Borre 24 animals by road	W.H.
	6.9.17		Evacuated to IX Corps M.V.D. 2 animals. One destroyed Butcher. 100 lbs required	W.H.

A6945 Wt. W11422/M1160 350,000 12/16 D. D. & L. Forms/C./2118/14.

Instructions regarding War Diaries and Intelligence Summaries are contained in F. S. Regs., Part II. and the Staff Manual respectively. Title pages will be prepared in manuscript.

WAR DIARY
or
INTELLIGENCE SUMMARY.
(Erase heading not required.)

Army Form C. 2118.

28TH MOBILE VETERINARY SECTION.
No. ......
Date ......

Place	Date	Hour	Summary of Events and Information	Remarks and references to Appendices
LOCRE	7.9.17		Admitted to section 4 animals, 1 evacuated	
			to IX corps. M.V.S.	W.H.
"	8.9.17		Admitted to section 7 animals, evacuated	
			to IX corps M.V.S. 2 animals	W.H.
"	9.9.17		Admitted to section 4 animals evacuated	
			to IX corps 3 animals. 1 animal returned	
			to unit cured. Received orders to move	
			to St Jans Capel new area. Handed over	
			1 animal to 31st M.V.S at LOCRE. 4	
			animals returned to unit cured	W.H.
St Jans Capel	10.9.17		Moved to St Jans Capel made men and	
			horses comfortable for the night.	W.H.
"	11.9.17		Admitted 23 animals, Rifle inspection.	
"	12.9.17		Admitted 8 animals evacuated 28 by	
"	"		Road to St Omer discharged 1 ~~to~~ duty,	
"	"		visited units usual section duties.	W.H.

A6945 Wt. W11422/M1160 350,000 12/16 D. D. & L. Forms/C./2118/14.

Instructions regarding War Diaries and Intelligence Summaries are contained in F. S. Regs., Part II, and the Staff Manual respectively. Title pages will be prepared in manuscript.

WAR DIARY
or
INTELLIGENCE SUMMARY.
(*Erase heading not required.*)

28TH MOBILE VETERINARY SECTION

Army Form C. 2118.

Place	Date	Hour	Summary of Events and Information	Remarks and references to Appendices
ST. JANS CAPEL	13-9-17		Usual section duties. [illegible] [illegible] of [illegible]	W.H.
"	14-9-17		admitted 18 animals Evacuated 13 to [illegible] by road discharged 1 to unit cured	W.H.
	15-9-17		Handed over section to Capt [illegible] on his return from leave	W.H.
"	16.9.17		2 animals admitted usual section duties DADVS called	[illegible]
"	17.9.17		Usual section duties weather fine 27 animals admitted 1 Discharged	
"	18.9.17		Weather dull 7 animals admitted. ADVS Corps called 50 animals from 2nd Army Sigs. billeted for the night with section	
"	19.9.17		Inspected Harness DADVS called, usual section duties weather fine admitted 5. 2 Discharged cured	
"	20.9.17		Usual section duties. 5 admitted 1 animal discharged weather fine	
	21.9.17		10 animals admitted 2 discharged cured DADVS called also ADVS	
	22.9.17		19 animals admitted 53 evacuated by road to St. Omer 2 discharged	
	23.9.17		3 " " 3 discharged usual section duties	
	24.9.17		13 " " 1 animal to butcher at BAILEUIL	

A6945 Wt. W11422/M1160 350,000 12/16 D. D. & L. Forms/C./2118/14.

Instructions regarding War Diaries and Intelligence Summaries are contained in F. S. Regs., Par. II. and the Staff Manual respectively. Title pages will be prepared in manuscript.

WAR DIARY
or
INTELLIGENCE SUMMARY.
(Erase heading not required.)

Army Form C. 2118.

Place	Date	Hour	Summary of Events and Information	Remarks and references to Appendices
St. JEAN. CAPEL.	25.9.17		Inspected Rifles & Harness usual section duties weather fine 2 animals admitted 1 discharged. D.A.D.V.S. Showed. 1 G.S. Limber & 1 N.C.O. rider at Divl. Show. which was held this day turnout very satisfactory: E.A. over Section.	JWY JWY
"	26.9.17.		21 Animals admitted, usual section duties. D.A.D.V.S called	JWY
"	27.9.17.		Visited units 23 animals admitted 8 discharged cured	
"	28.9.17		E.A. over section during night dropped 2 bombs in field next Section. wounding one of section men Pte. Wotherspoon.	JWY
"	29		Usual section duties evacuated 65 animals to St. OMER. also moved section to [illegible] LA CLYTTE. took over 25 Hides & 9 Float cases. move completed without incident	JWY
LA CLYTTE	30.9.17.		During night 3 bombs were dropped in section fortunately no damage 21 Cases were admitted, 2 discharged. D.A.D.V.S called	JWY
			During the month Section visited almost daily by D.A.D.V.S. 257 cases were admitted and 228 Evacuated by road to St. Omer. 59 animals discharged & 3 Destroyed	[illegible] Capt AVC O.C 28th M.V.S
			Section bombed 3 times by E.A. 1 man injured. places bombed "LOCRE" St. JEAN CAPPEL. and LA CLYTTE.	

Vol 25

War Diary

28th Mob. Vet. Section

Oct 1917

1/0/

37th Division "Q"

Herewith War Diary
for the month of October 1917

Captain AVC
O.C. 28th Mobile Veterinary Section

23TH
MOBILE VETERINARY
SECTION.
No. V 69
Date 2/11/17

Instructions regarding War Diaries and Intelligence Summaries are contained in F. S. Regs., Part. II. and the Staff Manual respectively. Title pages will be prepared in manuscript.

WAR DIARY
or
INTELLIGENCE SUMMARY.
(*Erase heading not required.*)

28TH MOBILE VETERINARY SECTION.
No. ......
Date......

Army Form C. 2118.

Place	Date	Hour	Summary of Events and Information	Remarks and references to Appendices
LA·CLYTTE.	1/10/17		Usual section duties, weather fine. E.A. over section bombs dropped (18) in immediate neighbourhood, 29 cases admitted to section all wounds from bombs 21 animals evacuated by Road to St. OMER.	[initials]
"	2.10.17.		Weather continues very fine A.D.V.S X corps. called 3 animal admitted two destroyed owing to shell wounds. Men returned from St. OMER.	[initials]
"	3.10.17		E.A. over Section during night. weather dull A.D.V.S. IX corps called 14 casualties admitted 2 Float cases sent to IX corps 1 animal died 1 destroyed	[initials]
"	4.10.17		Usual section duties. 4 casualties 1 cured & discharged. 1 destroyed weather dull	[initials]
"	5.10.17		4 Casualties Admitted 2 animals destroyed. 1 died weather broken. heavy showers	[initials]
"	6.10.17.		Usual section duties. Inspected rifles D.A.D.V.S. 31 animals admitted 1 destroyed. weather wet	[initials]
"	7.10.17		95 P.C. of animals in section suffering from wounds caused by bombs during the night. bomb dropped on road near section + wounded 3 section animals	[initials]
"	8.10.17		One animal admitted 61 animals evacuated by road to St. Omer 15 animals handed over to 12th M.V.S. Section moved from LA.CLYTTE. to SCHERPENBERG. Weather early part of day fine heavy rain night	[initials]

A6945 Wt. W11422/M1160 350,000 12/16 D. D. & L. Forms/C./2118/14.

Instructions regarding War Diaries and Intelligence Summaries are contained in F. S. Regs., Part II, and the Staff Manual respectively. Title pages will be prepared in manuscript.

WAR DIARY
or
INTELLIGENCE SUMMARY.
(Erase heading not required.)

28TH MOBILE VETERINARY SECTION.
No.........
Date.........

Army Form C. 2118.

Place	Date	Hour	Summary of Events and Information	Remarks and references to Appendices
SCHERPENBURG	9.10.17.		Tidied up camp DADVS called. Weather cold & wet. 1 animal discharged cured.	JWJ
"	10.10.17.		Usual routine work. Improved stables & cookhouse	JWJ
"	11.10.17.		8 animals admitted weather conditions bad.	JWJ
	12.10.17		Usual section duties. Men returned from St Omer, 8 animals admitted went with DADVS to WESTOUTRE to inspect Corps Clipping Shed	JWJ
	13.10.17		DADVS called. 11 animals admitted 2 discharged. Weather wet	JWJ
	14.10.17		Weather much improved 3 animals admitted. DADVS. 39 Div called	JWJ
	15.10.17		Weather continues fair DADVS went on leave. Section moved to St JEAN CAPPEL. 5 animals admitted 20 evacuated took over from 39 Divl Mobile	JWJ
St JEAN CAPEL	16.10.17		Usual section duties - lines in a very bad condition 2 animals discharged cured 3 admitted	JWJ
"	17.10.17		5 casualties admitted 1 discharged usual section duties 1 animal sold to Butcher	JWJ
"	18.10.17		15 animals admitted 1 sold to Butcher	
"	19.10.17		Usual section duties inspected harness & rifles.	JWJ

A6945 Wt. W11422/M1160 350,000 12/16 D. D. & L. Forms/C./2118/14.

Instructions regarding War Diaries and Intelligence Summaries are contained in F. S. Regs., Part II. and the Staff Manual respectively. Title pages will be prepared in manuscript.

WAR DIARY
or
INTELLIGENCE SUMMARY.
(Erase heading not required.)

23TH MOBILE VETERINARY SECTION.
No. ......
Date ......

Army Form C. 2118.

Place	Date	Hour	Summary of Events and Information	Remarks and references to Appendices
St JEAN. CAPEL	20.10.17		Evacuated 29 animals to St OMER by Road. weather much improved called Whee ADVS corps and went with him to inspect new clipping shed at LOCRE	[illegible]
"	" 21.10.17		Called at HQ re clipping of horses for the division and interviewed Q also went to LOCRE.	[illegible]
"	" 22.10.17		Usual section duties. visited units 12 animals admitted 1 discharged.	[illegible]
"	" 23.10.17		Visited Clipping Station + made arrangements to start divisional clipping	[illegible]
"	24.10.17		Took Staff Sgt + 2 men + started Divisional Clipping Depot at Locre. 4 animals admitted	[illegible]
"	25.10.17		Usual section duties 7 animals admitted 2 discharged cured visited Locre. Section moved to SCHAEXKEN	[illegible]
SCHAEXKEN	26.10.17		[illegible] Visited Locre, signed returns for DADVS usual section work 1 animal admitted 1 mule cured	[illegible]
"	27.10.17		6 animals admitted 31 sent by road to St OMER. 2 to IX Corps Detachment. DADVS returned from leave + handed over	[illegible]
"	28.10.17		6 animals admitted. went with DADVS to Locre	[illegible]
	29.10.17		3 animals admitted visited units usual section duties	

A6945 Wt. W11422/M1160 350,000 12/16 D. D. & L. Forms/C./2118/14.

Instructions regarding War Diaries and Intelligence Summaries are contained in F. S. Regs., Part II, and the Staff Manual respectively. Title pages will be prepared in manuscript.

WAR DIARY
or
INTELLIGENCE SUMMARY.
(Erase heading not required.)

23rd MOBILE VETERINARY SECTION.
No. ......
Date ......

Army Form C. 2118.

Place	Date	Hour	Summary of Events and Information	Remarks and references to Appendices
SCHAXKEN.	30.10.17.		Judged 112 Brigade for inter-brigade competition 3 admittions & 1 animal discharged cured weather cold & wet.	[illegible initials]
"	31.10.17		Usual section duties 1 animal admitted 1 animal sold to butcher for 125 francs.	[illegible initials]
			During the month the section moved 3 times.	
			D.A.D.V.S. went on leave & took over his duties.	
			165 animals were sent by road to base Hospital	Jno Hy Yates Capt AVC
			33 animals were discharge cured. 2 died &	O.C. 23rd M.V.S.
			11 destroyed. Started divisional clipping depot	
			at Locre.	

37th Divn. "Q"

Herewith War Diary for the month of November 1917.

[illegible]
Capt.
O.C. 28th M.V.S.

-28 MOBILE SECTION-
ARMY VETERINARY CORPS.
4/12/17

Instructions regarding War Diaries and Intelligence Summaries are contained in F. S. Regs., Part II, and the Staff Manual respectively. Title pages will be prepared in manuscript.

WAR DIARY
or
INTELLIGENCE SUMMARY.
(Erase heading not required.)

28 Mob Vety Sec
Vol 26

Army Form C. 2118.

Place	Date	Hour	Summary of Events and Information	Remarks and references to Appendices
SCHAEXKEN	1.11.17		Usual section duties. 4 casualties admitted. visited 9th NSR & 49th Field ambulance	
			called on DADVS. Weather fine	
"	2.11.17		Inspected rifles. 14 animals admitted 1 evacuated to 9th Corps DADVS called	
			Weather fine	
"	3.11.17		26 animals evacuated by Road to St. Omer. 1 to IX Corps Mobile 1 Mule sent to	
"			11th Warwicks Paid section & also paid Field Cashier 300 francs for 2 animals Sold	
"	4.11.17		Weather fine sent 1 animal to Corps (IX) Mobile Usual section duties visited units	
"	5.11.17		Started clipping section horses 2 casualties admitted visited units re	
"	6.11.17		Weather dull. 4 animals admitted. OC 31st MVS called reference to taking over	
			place.	
"	7.11.17		Usual Section Schedule 3 animals admitted DADVS called visited units. destroyed 1	
"	8.11.17		5 animals admitted. Visited LOCRE made arrangements to take over DADVS called	
"	9.11.17		Inspected Harness usual section duties. Destroyed Tetanus case	
"	10.11.17		admitted 10 horses + 1 Mule. Evacuated by Road to St. OMER. 11 Horses + 1 Mule	
			1 Horse discharged. Section moved to LOCRE.	
LOCRE	11.10.17		Usual section duties. 1 animal evacuated to Corps MVS. admitted 5 animals	

A6945 Wt. W11422/M1160 350,000 12/16 D. D. & L. Forms/C./2118/14.

Army Form C. 2118.

Instructions regarding War Diaries and Intelligence Summaries are contained in F. S. Regs., Par. II. and the Staff Manual respectively. Title pages will be prepared in manuscript.

WAR DIARY
or
INTELLIGENCE SUMMARY.
(Erase heading not required.)

Place	Date	Hour	Summary of Events and Information	Remarks and references to Appendices
LOCRE	12.11.17		9 Casualties admitted 1 discharged cured 1 evacuated. weather cold & wet	
"	13.11.17		13 animals admitted. Inspected Harness. DADVS called evacuated to St OMER 16 Horses + 7 mules. + to IX Corps M. 4 animals.	JM
"	14.11.17		DADVS called visited units & examined scrapings. usual section duties 1 animal admitted 12 evacuated to IX corps	JM
"	15.11.17		Inspected Rifles 4 admittions 2 evacuated DADVS called	
"	16.11.17		Usual section duties 4 — do — — do —	JM
"	17.11.17		Visited DAC & other units. 3 animals clipped usual section work	
"	18.11.17		2 Horses 9 mules admitted DADVS called inspected rifles	JM
"	19.11.17		Usual section duties 12 Horses 6 mules admitted visits units 1 animal evacuated 1 mule discharged	
"	20.11.17		Usual section duties 1 mules admitted. 27 Horses 10 mules to St OMER 2 Mules to IX Corps Det.	JM
"	21.11.17		Usual Section work. 2 animals admitted. 2 animals evacuated 1 discharged.	JM
"	22.11.17		Visited units. 6 animals admitted 1 Mule evacuated 1 Horse discharged	JM

A6945 Wt. W11422/M1160 350,000 12/16 D. D. & L. Forms/C./2118/14.

Instructions regarding War Diaries and Intelligence Summaries are contained in F. S. Regs., Part. II. and the Staff Manual, respectively. Title pages will be prepared in manuscript.

WAR DIARY
or
INTELLIGENCE SUMMARY.
(Erase heading not required.)

Army Form C. 2118.

Place	Date	Hour	Summary of Events and Information	Remarks and references to Appendices
LOCRE	23.11.17		Visited units 1 animal admitted 1 evacuated. improved camp.	
"	24.11.17		9 animals admitted 2 animals evacuated. weather fine Section visited by DADVS	JH
"	25.11.17		Inspected mens kit etc painted transport 14 Horses & 3 mules admitted	JH
"	26.11.17		Usual work in section 20 animals admitted 6 horses 1 mule evacuated visited 2nd ZANAC MVS with DADVS	
"	27.11.17		Inspected rifles 14 horses admitted evacuated ~~40~~ 6 + 6 from IX Corps Section moved to LA CLYTTE.	JH
LA CLYTTE	28.11.17		Cleared up camp 6 animals admitted 6 to ~~[illegible]~~ ZANAC Corps. DADVS Called	
"	29.11.17		Visited units. + H.Q. 1 Horses destroyed collected 1 animal from IX Corps H.Q.	JH
"	30.11.17		13 animals admitted evacuated 10 to other mobile. During the month the section was visited daily by DADVS 43 float cases were dealt with. 219 animals were admitted 192 animals were evacuated 9 animals were returned cured to their unit	JHopkins Capt AVC O.C. 28th MVS

A6945 Wt. W11422/M1160 350,000 12/16 D. D. & L. Forms/C./2118/14.

28th Mob Vet Section

Instructions regarding War Diaries and Intelligence Summaries are contained in F. S. Regs., Part II, and the Staff Manual respectively. Title pages will be prepared in manuscript.

WAR DIARY
or
INTELLIGENCE SUMMARY.
(Erase heading not required.)

Army Form C. 2118.

Vol 27

Place	Date	Hour	Summary of Events and Information	Remarks and references to Appendices
LA.CLYTTE	1-12-17		Usual section duties 9 hrs 14 mule admitted evacuated 1 discharged 2	
"	2.12.17		Visited units 16 animals admitted 2 destroyed	
"	3 12.17		16 Ho: 3 Mules admitted evacuated 69.	
"	4 12 17		Usual section work improved camp. DADVS frequently called	
	to		40 animals admitted 3 discharged. visited units.	
	9.12 17		built up cookhouse etc.	
	10.12.17		19 admission. 43 animals evacuated 2 discharged	
	11 12.17		GOC visited section as well as Corps ADVS 3 animals	
			admitted 1 evacuated 1 discharged 1 destroyed	
"	12.12.17		to 13 12.17. 23 animals admitted 1 to Butcher	
	14 12.17		Section moved to KRABBENHOFF. FARM LOCRE	
LOCRE	15th 12.17		to 16.12.17. 33 animals admitted 7 discharged	
	17.12.17		7 admitted evacuated 66 animals. 1 Ho to butcher	
	18 12.17		4 animals admitted improved camp built forage place	
			etc. 1 animal to butcher 1 discharged	
	19.12.17		to 21.12.17 Evacuated 7 animals + admitted 6. 1 discharged	

A6945 Wt. W11422/M1160 35,000 12/16 D. D. & L. Forms/C./2118/14.

Instructions regarding War Diaries and Intelligence Summaries are contained in F. S. Regs., Part II, and the Staff Manual respectively. Title pages will be prepared in manuscript.

WAR DIARY
or
INTELLIGENCE SUMMARY.
(Erase heading not required.)

Army Form C. 2118.

Place	Date	Hour	Summary of Events and Information	Remarks and references to Appendices
LOCRE	20-12-17		Usual section duties DADVS called visited units. 2 casualties admitted	[illegible]
"	21-12-17		Inspected Rifles Improved camp. 1 animal cured 10 men AVC arrived	
"			from base to replace Class A men of section 4 animals admitted.	[illegible]
"	22-12-17		~~[illegible]~~ 14 animals admitted 2 evacuated to V.C.C.S. weather cold	[illegible]
"	23-12-17		Visited units Men of section had Xmas dinner DADVS called Weather very cold	[illegible]
La Clytte	24-12-17		6 Horses 1 Mule admitted 27 Horses 1 Mule evacuated to VCCS Section moved to LA CLYTTE. 10 class A men from section sent to Base.	[illegible]
"	25-12-17		Xmas Day. Saw animal at D/123 RFA DADVS called weather cold & showery	
"	26-12-17		Usual section duties 3 animals admitted 1 Horse evacuated weather still cold	[illegible]
"	27-12-17		Inspected harness etc visited units. 12 animals admitted 1 cured	
"	28-12-17		1 Horse admitted 16 animals evacuated 1 destroyed. 22 [illegible] cases in Section	DADVS visited [illegible]
"	29-12-17		Handed over Section to Capt. Beaumont whilst on leave	
	"		12 animals admitted, 2 cured & 2 destroyed.	R.L.B.
La Clytte	30-12-17		3 animals admitted, usual section duties. D.D.V.S. called	R.L.B.
	31-12-17		12 " " "	R.L.B.

A6945 Wt. W11422/M1160 350,000 12/16 D. D. & L. Forms/C./2118/14.

Instructions regarding War Diaries and Intelligence Summaries are contained in F. S. Regs., Par. II, and the Staff Manual respectively. Title pages will be prepared in manuscript.

WAR DIARY
or
INTELLIGENCE SUMMARY.
(Erase heading not required.)

Army Form C. 2118.

28 Mob Vety Sec

Vol 28

Place	Date	Hour	Summary of Events and Information	Remarks and references to Appendices
LA CLYTTE	1-1-18.		Admitted 3 animals, D.A.D.V.S. called	R.L.B.
" "	2-1-18		Evacuated 25 animals " "	R.L.B.
" "	3-1-18		Admitted 2 animals, sent to 7 C.C.S.	R.L.B.
" "	4-1-18		" " , D.A.D.V.S. called	R.L.B.
" "	5-1-18		" 8 " cured 6 animals " "	R.L.B.
" "	6-1-18		One animal cured, D.A.D.V.S. called	R.L.B.
" "	7-1-18		Admitted 5, evacuated one, discharged one	R.L.B.
" "	8-1-18		Admitted 2 " D.A.D.V.S. called	R.L.B.
" "	9-1-18		Admitted 4 " "	R.L.B.
" "	10-1-18		Evacuated 27 animals, paid Section & handed over to Lieut. Craig	R.L.B.
	11.1.18	©	Section moved to STRAZEELE.	
	12.1.18		Section moved to RACQUINGHEM.	
	13.1.18		Evacuated 13 remount cases. to 23 V.H.	
	14.1.18		Capt. YATES. reported from leave & took over Section. 1 animal collected by DADVS & sent to Section	

A6945 Wt. W11422/M1160 350,000 12/16 D. D. & L. Forms/C./2118/14.

Instructions regarding War Diaries and Intelligence Summaries are contained in F. S. Regs., Part II. and the Staff Manual respectively. Title pages will be prepared in manuscript.

WAR DIARY
or
INTELLIGENCE SUMMARY.
(Erase heading not required.)

Army Form C. 2118.

Place	Date	Hour	Summary of Events and Information	Remarks and references to Appendices
RACQUINHEM.	15.1.18		1 animal admitted weather cold and wet. DADVS visited section	JH
"	16.1.18		Visited units. Staff Sgt reported back overstayed his leave 2 days	JH
"	17.1.18		1 Mule admitted visited all units in 111 Brigade + 48th Field ambulance	
"			1762 RE.	
"	18.1.18		1 H.D from 13 KRR climatic conditions cold + wet visited 9th NSR Transport	JH
"	19.1.18.		5 Horses + 3 mules admitted. 5 animals sent by road to St OMER V.H	JH
"			3 section men went on leave.	
"	20.1.18.		1 animal from 37 Signals admitted, evacuated by road 3H + 3M by road	JH
"			Visited 3/6 of Train.	
"	21.1.18		1 Mule admitted. 2 animals evacuated weather conditions fair	JH
"	22.1.18		Weather condition fair visited 13th RF + 3/6 Train + other units. Usual Sect. work	
"	23.1.18.		Inspected rifles. read fire orders. 3 animals admitted took over duties of	JH
"	24.1.18		A/DADVS. 2 animals admitted 3 evacuated	
"	25.1.18		Visited units + H.Q. 1 admitted. Usual section work.	JH
	26.1.18		Visited H.Q. DADVS Office + etc Usual section work	JH
	27.1.18		Visited units 1 animal admitted climatic conditions good + ok	JH

A6945 Wt. W11422/M1160 350,000 12/16 D. D. & L. Forms/C./2118/14.

Instructions regarding War Diaries and Intelligence Summaries are contained in F. S. Regs., Part II, and the Staff Manual respectively. Title pages will be prepared in manuscript.

WAR DIARY
or
INTELLIGENCE SUMMARY.
(Erase heading not required.)

Army Form C. 2118.

Place	Date	Hour	Summary of Events and Information	Remarks and references to Appendices
RACQUINHAM.	28.1.18		1 animal evacuated inspected harness & visited various units.	
"	29.1.18		Called at H.Q. & attended to duties of D.A.D.V.S. Usual section work.	
"	30.1.18		Evacuated 2 animals to Base Hospital weather conditions fair	
"	31.1.18		Made out returns visited H.Q. and units [illegible]	
			[illegible] Capt A.V.C.	
			O.C. 28th Mobile Veterinary Section.	

A6945 Wt. W11422/M1160 350,000 12/16 D. D. & L. Forms/C./2118/14.

16

WAR DIARY
or
INTELLIGENCE SUMMARY.
(Erase heading not required.)

28th Mob Vet Sect
37 D
Vol 29

Army Form C. 2118.

Instructions regarding War Diaries and Intelligence Summaries are contained in F. S. Regs., Par. II. and the Staff Manual respectively. Title pages will be prepared in manuscript.

Place	Date	Hour	Summary of Events and Information	Remarks and references to Appendices
RACQUINGHEM	1/2/18		One animal admitted, visited units also H.Q. attended [illegible] made PM	[illegible]
"	2.2.18		Two admissions visited units weather conditions very good all transport was painted during last week	[initials]
"	3.2.18 to 6.2.18		3 animals admitted 2 evacuated. visited units daily also DADVS Office & sent in returns & answered correspondence	[initials]
	7.2.18 to 15.2.18		6 Horses & 3 mules admitted 4 horses 3 mules evacuated, 2 Horses discharged. had all transport painted Section inspected by DADVS	[initials]
	16.2.18		Section moved to STRAZEELE	[initials]
WESTOUTRE	17.2.18		Section moved to WESTOUTRE. took over two animals from 32 MVS	[initials]
	18.2.18		Usual section work one animal admitted visited units with DADVS	[initials]
	19.2.18		Started to improve camp, section work 9 animals admitted	[initials]
	20.2.18		5 animals admitted new man joined unit	
	21.2.18		1 animal admitted visited units [illegible] 10 animals evacuated by rail	[initials]

A6945 Wt. W11422/M1160 350,000 12/16 D. D. & L. Forms/C./2118/14.

Instructions regarding War Diaries and Intelligence Summaries are contained in F. S. Regs., Par. II, and the Staff Manual respectively. Title pages will be prepared in manuscript.

WAR DIARY
or
INTELLIGENCE SUMMARY.
(Erase heading not required.)

Army Form C. 2118.

Place	Date	Hour	Summary of Events and Information	Remarks and references to Appendices
WESTOUTRE	22.2.18.		Usual Section duties visited units 1 animal admitted	[illegible]
"	23.2.18.		Improved stables etc 1 animal admitted 1 evacuated cured.	[illegible]
"	24.2.18.		Usual section work. Inspected rifles 3 animals admitted	[illegible]
"	25.2.18		Visited units 1 animal admitted	[illegible]
"	26.2.18		7 animals admitted, visited units + usual ~~[illegible]~~ section work	[illegible]
"	27.2.18.		3 animals admitted 1 died evacuated 13 animals.	[illegible]
			During the month carried on duties of DADVS who was on	[illegible]
			leave. section moved from rest area. Cleaned up new camp	[illegible]
			+ salvaged S.S. lumber of various articles etc	
			[illegible] Capt. AVC	
			O.C. 28th MVS	

A6945 Wt. W11422/M1160 350,000 12/16 D. D. & L. Forms/C./2118/14.

To 37th Divn. Q.

16

Herewith 28th M.V.S. War diary for month ending 31.3.'18.

1.4.18

[illegible] Capt.
O.C. 28th M.V.S

Instructions regarding War Diaries and Intelligence Summaries are contained in F. S. Regs., Par. II. and the Staff Manual respectively. Title pages will be prepared in manuscript.

WAR DIARY
or
INTELLIGENCE SUMMARY.
(Erase heading not required.)

Army Form C. 2118.

28 Mob Vety Sec.
37 Div
Vol 30

Place	Date	Hour	Summary of Events and Information	Remarks and references to Appendices
WESTOUTRE	1·3·18 to 6·3·18		Usual section duties improve stables cookhouses & roadway, visited units etc 10 animals admitted to section weather conditions during this period fairly good.	
"	7·3·18 to 14·3·18		During this period 25 animals admitted to section and 28 animals evacuated to base hospital. ADVS of Corps visited Section DADVS of division also. 4 animals returned to units cured	
"	15·3·18 to 21·3·18		Usual section & office work visited units 17 animals admitted and 10 evacuated. made 3 loose boxes also dark box for Ophthalmia cases.	
	22·3·18 to 27·3·18		During this period weather was much cooler erected mess room for men. 23 animals admitted, 25 animals evacuated 12 animals discharged to units cured 2 destroyed. Section moved to Godsveeldt	
GODSVEELDT	28·3·17.		Section stationary awaiting instructions saw Staff Capt of 112 & 63 Groups re same	
"	29·3·17.		Section entrained for MONDICOURT. ~~[illegible]~~ at 3 A.M.	
TOUTENCOURT	30·3·17		Detrained and marched Section to TOUTENCOURT. afterwards moved Section to ~~[illegible]~~ FRANCHON	

A6945 Wt. W11422/M1160 350,000 12/16 D. D. & L. Forms/C./2118/14.

Instructions regarding War Diaries and Intelligence Summaries are contained in F. S. Regs., Part II. and the Staff Manual respectively. Title pages will be prepared in manuscript.

WAR DIARY
or
INTELLIGENCE SUMMARY.
(Erase heading not required.)

Army Form C. 2118.

Place	Date	Hour	Summary of Events and Information	Remarks and references to Appendices
FAMECHON	31.3.18		Usual section duties. 5 animals admitted: 1 a stray. Section managed to get under cover weather conditions warm and fine during the month. DADVS frequently visited section. Improved camp. This section ~~[illegible]~~ landed in France 31-7-15.	
			Jno Hy Yates Capt AVC O.C. 28th MVS 31-3-18	

A6945 Wt. W11422/M1160 350,000 12/16 D. D. & L. Forms/C./2118/14.

To

37th Division "A"

Herewith War Diary of 28th M. V. S. for Month of April 1918.

[signature]

Capt AVC

2/5/18 OC 28th Mob Vety Section

Army Form C. 2118.

Instructions regarding War Diaries and Intelligence Summaries are contained in F. S. Regs., Part II. and the Staff Manual respectively. Title pages will be prepared in manuscript.

WAR DIARY
or
INTELLIGENCE SUMMARY.
(Erase heading not required.)

-28 MOBILE SECTION- ARMY VETERINARY CORPS

Place	Date	Hour	Summary of Events and Information	Remarks and references to Appendices
FAMECHON	1.4.18		Usual section duties. evacuated 5 animals. Went to DOULLENS. with sick	[illegible]
"	2.4.18.		Routine work DADVS called 8 casualties admitted. visited units. removed section to better quarters	[illegible]
"	3.4.18.		5 casualties admitted evacuated 9 to DOULLENS. by road visited DAC. 4, 3 Sects	
"	4.4.18.		Usual section & office work admitted 10 casualties. 5 evacuated visited HQ and saw DADVS made up returns. Weather conditions bad rain continuous	[illegible]
"	5.4.18		26 animals admitted sick to section. 1 animal discharged cured 11 evacuated by road to V.E.S. weather bad	[illegible]
"	6.4.18		4 animals admitted 22 animals evacuated 1 destroyed held rifle inspection sent collected salvage to dump.	[illegible]
"	7.4.18.		Usual section duties weather conditions improved called at HQ 5 saw DADVS about various matters	[illegible]
"	8.4.18		8 animals admitted & evacuated. usual section duties.	[illegible]
"	9.4.18		A.D.V.S. Corps called. treated two cows belonging to French	[illegible]
"	10.4.18		Usual section duties. inspection of Bot respirators 4 casualties admitted DADVS called	[illegible]

A6945 Wt. W11422/M1160 350,000 12/16 D. D. & L. Forms/C./2118/14.

Instructions regarding War Diaries and Intelligence Summaries are contained in F. S. Regs., Par. II, and the Staff Manual respectively. Title pages will be prepared in manuscript.

WAR DIARY
or
INTELLIGENCE SUMMARY.
(Erase heading not required.)

Army Form C. 2118.

Place	Date	Hour	Summary of Events and Information	Remarks and references to Appendices
FRAMECHON	11.4.18.		Usual section duties. Office routine 4 casualties admitted 8 evacuated 1 death hide recovered.	[illegible]
"	12.4.18		Rifle inspection improved standings section duties 4 animals admitted	[illegible]
St LEGER. L'AUTHIE	13.4.18		After evacuating 7 animals section moved to this place. 2 discharged animals in open 7 men in trench shelters. weather very fine	[illegible]
"	14.4.18		Usual section work DADVS called. evacuated 3 animals 1 admitted	[illegible]
"	15.4.18		Improved lines weather ~~cool~~ cold. 5 admitted evacuated 2	
"	16.4.18		Usual section work. called at DADVS Office admitted 3 evacuated 2 discharged 4 fit for duty.	[illegible]
"	17.4.18		Routine work 8 animals admitted evacuated 11 animals	
"	18.4.18		Weather conditions bad very cold. Inspected Box respirators changed lines etc	[illegible]
"	19.4.18		Usual section duties weather cold some snow admitted 2 evacuated 4	[illegible]
AUTHIE	20.4.18		DADVS called admitted 2 evacuated 3 Section moved	
"	21.4.18		Usual routine work admitted 8 evacuated 10 weather improved	[illegible]
	22.4.18		Inspected Box respirators by Gas Sergeant. 9 animals admitted	[illegible]

Instructions regarding War Diaries and Intelligence Summaries are contained in F. S. Regs., Part. II, and the Staff Manual respectively. Title pages will be prepared in manuscript.

WAR DIARY
or
INTELLIGENCE SUMMARY
(Erase heading not required.)

Army Form C. 2118.

Place	Date	Hour	Summary of Events and Information	Remarks and references to Appendices
AUTHIE	23.4.18		Usual section duties. 8 casualties admitted. 1 animal destroyed. 7 evacuated.	JMY
"	24.4.18		Inspected saddler & harness etc. 9 cases admitted. 5 evacuated & 1 died. Usual works	JMY
"	25.4.18		Weather better but cold. 10 admitted. 4 evacuated by road to V.E.S.	JMY
"	26.4.18		Inspected rifles. DADVS called. 6 animals admitted. 9 to V.E.S. 1 discharged to duty. 1 died	JMY
"	27.4.18		16 casualties admitted. 4 to VES. Usual section work & visited units	JMY
"	28.4.18		Usual section duties. 3 animals admitted. 15 evacuated. 1 discharged for duty. M.V.S. used as place for examination of cold shoers. Appointed to the board	JMY
"	29.4.18		4 animals admitted. Evacuated 3. Carried on with examination of cold shoers	JMY
"	30.4.18		3 animals admitted. Evacuated 2. Completed examination of candidates for shoeing smiths. 13 passed the test out of 29. 2 only being absentees. Test of making shoes very difficult & being the cause of most of the failures. During the month DADVS called almost daily. 191 animals admitted during the month. 160 evacuated. 12 discharged to duty. 3 destroyed. 2 died. Remainder in Section. During the month 20 loads of chalk & 20 loads of cinders were lead to section for improvement of standings & yard, & other improvements made.	JMY

J M Yates Capt
O.C. 28th M.V.S

A6945 Wt. W11422/M1160 350,000 12/16 D. D. & L. Forms/C./2118/14.

Instructions regarding War Diaries and Intelligence Summaries are contained in F. S. Regs., Par. II. and the Staff Manual respectively. Title pages will be prepared in manuscript.

Army Form C. 2118.

WAR DIARY
or
INTELLIGENCE SUMMARY.
(Erase heading not required.)

Place	Date	Hour	Summary of Events and Information	Remarks and references to Appendices
AUTHIE	30.4.18.		Reference A.G. Base 17/259/18.A. Date of mobilization of the Division. April 19. 1915. Formation of Mobile Veterinary Section same date.	
			Date of proceeding over seas from U.K. 31-7-15.	
			B. W. Known.	
			[signature] Capt. AVC	

A6945 Wt. W11422/M1160 350,000 12/16 D. D. & L. Forms/C./2118/14.

11 37

Instructions regarding War Diaries and Intelligence Summaries are contained in F. S. Regs., Part. II, and the Staff Manual respectively. Title pages will be prepared in manuscript.

WAR DIARY
or
INTELLIGENCE SUMMARY.
(Erase heading not required.)

28 Mob Vety Sec

Army Form C. 2118.

Vol 32

Place	Date	Hour	Summary of Events and Information	Remarks and references to Appendices
AUTHIE	1.5.18		Usual section duties + office work. visited units + attended to several	
"	to		French civilian animals. during this period 43 animals were admitted	
"	7.5.18		and 34 evacuated. 3 discharged to units + 4 animals destroyed	
"	8.5.18		During this period the section was visited by D.A.D.V.S also by	
"	to		A.D.V.S. IV Corps usual routine work was carried out. 37 casualties	
"	12.5.18		were admitted to section 31 evacuated 6 animals discharged	
"	13.5.18		Yesterday Capt Stewart A.V.C was temporarily attached to the section	
			+ today 20. O.R. also. pending a place being found for a V.E.S	
			in Corps area. during the night building occupied by M.V.S + 62nd	
	to		H.Q animals collapsed burying 20 animals. All were rescued	
			without injuries of any consequence. Sgt Bevan. Pte McAllister and	
			Pte Walker acted with coolness + courage in the extraction of	
	19.5.18		the animals. Visited units 63 casualties were admitted 43 evacuated	
			2 discharged. The weather during this time much improved. the last	
			4 days being exceeding warm. most of the section horses have been	
			out grazing during the day	

A6945 Wt. W11422/M1160 350,000 12/16 D. D. & L. Forms/C./2118/14.

Instructions regarding War Diaries and Intelligence Summaries are contained in F. S. Regs., Par. II. and the Staff Manual respectively. Title pages will be prepared in manuscript.

WAR DIARY
or
INTELLIGENCE SUMMARY.
(Erase heading not required.)

Army Form C. 2118.

Place	Date	Hour	Summary of Events and Information	Remarks and references to Appendices
AUTHIE	20.5.18 to 25.5.18		During this period weather conditions were extraordinary good. 35 animals were admitted to section 48 evacuated 4 discharged and 1 destroyed.	
	26.5.18 to 31.5.18		Usual section duties and office work. nothing of much importance to note considering the amt. of bombing by E.A. few casualties in our division. 30 casualties [illegible] admitted. 23 evacuated to 4 VES. by road 10 animals discharged. 1 destroyed. Section visited by A.D.V.S. corps and daily by DADVS	

Jno W. [illegible] Capt
AVC
OC 28th MVS

A6945 Wt. W11422/M1160 350,000 12/16 D. D. & L. Forms/C./2118/14.

Instructions regarding War Diaries and Intelligence Summaries are contained in F. S. Regs., Par. II. and the Staff Manual respectively. Title pages will be prepared in manuscript.

WAR DIARY
or
INTELLIGENCE SUMMARY.
(Erase heading not required.)

Army Form C. 2118.

Place	Date	Hour	Summary of Events and Information	Remarks and references to Appendices
AUTHIE.	1·6·18		Usual section duties weather conditions very good during this period 7	
to			animals were admitted to section and 13 evacuated by road to	
"	3·6·18.		4 V.E.S.	
"	4·6·18		Cleared section of sick animals 2 discharged to units 8 evacuated	
			left AUTHIE 9 P.M. and arrived WARGNIES. 6 AM. on the 5.	
WARGNIES	5·6·18		Section rested most of the day. reported to C.R.A. arrival & visited neighbouring units	
			left WARGNIES. 9 P.M. and arrived BREILLY 5 AM. on the 6th	
BREILLY	6·6·18		Rested during the morning took over lines from No. 1 Co Train after	
			noon remainder of day occupied making horse troughs sanitation etc	
"	7·6·18		found room for Office established same section duties proceeded with	
" to	8·6·18		6 animals were admitted 15 evacuated to VES. DADVS called	
"	9·6·18		Usual routine work admitted 2 animals evacuated 3 to 19 VES	
			thus clearing section & made preparations for move at short notice	
"	10·6·18		left BREILLY at 10 AM. destination unknown but arrived	
			at PLACHY-BUYON eventually with III GROUP. struck camp	
			and reported situation to H.Q. & DADVS supplies etc.	

A6945 Wt. W14422/M1160 350,000 12/16 D. D. & L. Forms/C./2118/14.

17

Instructions regarding War Diaries and Intelligence Summaries are contained in F. S. Regs., Par. II. and the Staff Manual respectively. Title pages will be prepared in manuscript.

WAR DIARY
or
INTELLIGENCE SUMMARY.
(Erase heading not required.)

Army Form C. 2118.

28 Mob Vety Sec

Vol 33

Place	Date	Hour	Summary of Events and Information	Remarks and references to Appendices
PLACHY-BUYON.	11.6.18. to 16.6.18		Established section at this place 7 casualties were admitted 2 evacuated built protecting wall round horse lines. S.A.D.V.S called almost daily took over charge of units in neighbourhood until French DADVS	
"	17.6.18 to 20.6.18		During this period usual office work & section duties 7 animals admitted to section 2 cured 6 evacuated section moved	
FIESSELLES.	21.6.18		Section arrived here without incident & struck camp for night	
TERRAMASNIL	22.6.18		Remained here this day.	
PAS	23.6.18		Received orders to move section here arrived noon	
	24.6.18 to 30.6.18		Established M.V.S on PAS – MONDICOURT road. during this period 22 animals admitted 21 evacuated 1 cured to unit.	

[signature] Capt AVC
O.C. 28th M.V.S.

A6945 Wt. W11422/M1160 350,000 12/16 D. D. & L. Forms/C./2118/14.

19

Army Form C. 2118.

Instructions regarding War Diaries and Intelligence Summaries are contained in F. S. Regs., Part II, and the Staff Manual respectively. Title pages will be prepared in manuscript.

WAR DIARY
or
INTELLIGENCE SUMMARY.
(Erase heading not required.)

28 Mob Vety Sec

Vol 34

Place	Date	Hour	Summary of Events and Information	Remarks and references to Appendices
PAS.	1.7.18		3 horses and 3 mules were admitted to Section. Section Duties in forenoon & to Town to Field Cashier in afternoon, with no result. DADVS visited Section	
"	2.7.18		Three horses admitted. 4 animals evacuated to 4th VES. Paid Section. Weather beautiful	
"	3.7.18		Five admissions. Visited Units of which I have Vety charge.	
"	4.7.18		Three admissions. 7 animals evacuated. Compiled weekly returns & attended DADVS Conference.	
"	5.7.18		Section Duties. Forenoon to 410th Labour Coy. 10 sick animals admitted 1 discharged to Unit	
"	6.7.18 to 10/7/18		31 admissions. 32 animals evacuated to 4th V.E.S. 4 discharged cured to Units. 1 HD died on 8/7/18 from Intestinal trouble. 2 mules destroyed (Shell wounds)	
"	11/7/18		Morning spent visiting Units after which completed weekly returns & attended conference at DADVS office. admitted 8 animals & evacuated 7 to V.E.S	
"	12/7/18 & 13/7/18		Two admissions. 8 evacuated to V.E.S. Section duties performed.	
"	14/7/18		Weather showery. Usual duties carried out. Prepared to accept about 20 animals for evacuation from 2/1st (W.R.) M.V.S. 62nd Divn which are moving out.	

A6945 Wt. W11422/M1160 350,000 12/16 D. D. & L. Forms/C./2118/14.

Instructions regarding War Diaries and Intelligence Summaries are contained in F. S. Regs., Part II. and the Staff Manual respectively. Title pages will be prepared in manuscript.

WAR DIARY
or
INTELLIGENCE SUMMARY.
(*Erase heading not required.*)

Army Form C. 2118.

Place	Date	Hour	Summary of Events and Information	Remarks and references to Appendices
PAS.	15/7/18		Took over 19 animals from 2/1st (W.R.) M.V.S at 3. am. Evacuated 16 of them & three from my lines at 5.30 am. Demanded motor ambulance for two of former. One kept in Section under observation. Building forge &c began with material left by 62nd M.V.S. admitted 20 sick animals	
"	16/7/18		Evacuated 17 by road to 4th V.E.S. Motor Ambulce arrived & took two held over yesterday. 3 animals admitted. G.O.C. Division visited Section lines. Capt Martin paid Section for me as I did not feel well.	
"	17/7/18		Evacuated 2 sick animals to 4th V.E.S. Motor Ambulance arrived & took over float cases away, leaving Section practically clear. Later 10 cases were admitted.	
"	18/7/18		Admitted 8 animals. Evacuated 5. Discharged 1 to Unit cured. Visited Units compiled weekly returns & attended Conference at DADVS office. Prepared to proceed on leave. Handed everything over to Capt. Martin A.V.C.	
"	19/7/18 to 25/7/18		The admissions during the week totalled 39. Evacuations totalled 34. 4 were discharged cured to Units. Weather unsettled. Frequent visits were made by DADVS.	
"	26/7/18 to 31/7/18		47 animals admitted. 44 evacuated to Evacuating Station. 9 discharged cured or re-issued. Sections were paid on 28/7/18. Daily visits to Section by DADVS. Weather rainy during the period.	

A6945 Wt. W11422/M1160 350,000 12/16 D. D. & L. Forms/C./2118/14.

J Martin Capt. O.C. 28th Mobile Vety Section

17

WAR DIARY
or
INTELLIGENCE SUMMARY.
(Erase heading not required.)

Instructions regarding War Diaries and Intelligence Summaries are contained in F. S. Regs., Part. II. and the Staff Manual respectively. Title pages will be prepared in manuscript.

Army Form C. 2118.

28 Mob Vety Sec

V.R. 34

37

Place	Date	Hour	Summary of Events and Information	Remarks and references to Appendices
PAS EN ARTOIS	1.8.18.		The month commenced mild but showery. Evacuated 4 animals to Evacuating Station. Discharged one cured to Unit. Prepared weekly returns & attended DADVS conference.	
"	2.8.18		ADVS 4th Corps visited Section during the morning with DADVS Division. One mule admitted & one horse evacuated. The admission being from USARMY.	
"	3.8.18		Seven admissions. Mule from USARMY destroyed & buried (hide recovered). Weather still unsettled.	
"	4.8.18		Seven admissions. Evacuated 6 animals to VES. Capt Yates returned from leave this evening.	
"	5.8.18		Handed over Section & cases under treatment to Capt. Yates. Seven admissions. Evacuated six to VES.	
"	6.8.18 to 10.8.18		Admitted 16 animals. Evacuated 23. Cured 1 & re-issued to Unit. 4 American OR of Vety Corps arrived 7/8/18 to be attached for rations & instructions in duties of an MVS.	
"	11.8.18 to 15.8.18		44 Admissions. 30 Evacuated. 7 re-issued to Units fit for duty. Frequent visits by DADVS	
"	16.8.18 to 22.8.18		Admitted 52 animals 46 evacuated. 6 discharged to Units of Div. Major Stevenson proceeded to England 19/8/18 on month's leave. Major J. Connell, AVC took over duties of DADVS 21/8/18. DVS & Staff visited Section 22/8/18 & expressed satisfaction.	

A6945 Wt. W11422/M1160 35,000 12/16 D. D. & L. Forms/C./2118/14.

Instructions regarding War Diaries and Intelligence Summaries are contained in F. S. Regs., Par. II. and the Staff Manual respectively. Title pages will be prepared in manuscript.

WAR DIARY
or
INTELLIGENCE SUMMARY.
(Erase heading not required.)

Army Form C. 2118.

Place	Date	Hour	Summary of Events and Information	Remarks and references to Appendices
PAS-en-ARTOIS	23.8.18 to 25/8/18		33 admissions. 16 evacuated to VES. 2 discharged. 1 Died & buried (Hide recovered) also 1 destroyed (Hide recovered) Received orders & prepared to move early morning of 26/8/18	
"	26.8.18		Evacuated 20 animals at 5. am. Evacuated billet at PAS & proceeded to FONQUEVILLERS where the day was spent. 3 admissions were handed over to 5th M.V.S.	
FONQUEVILLERS	27/8/18.		Reveille 4. am. Moved off to LOGEAST WOOD 6. am where we prepared to spend some days. Admitted 2 cases. Issued a stray mule to 13th R.B.	
LOGEAST WOOD	28/8/18 to 31/8/18.		Admitted 23 casualties. Evacuated 15 to VES. Discharged 2 animals. One horse died from shell wounds & one was destroyed for same reason. Hides were removed & carcases buried. DADVS visited Unit daily	

Jno Hy Yates Capt
O.C. 28th M.V.S.
31-8-18.

A6945 Wt. W11422/M1160 350,000 12/16 D. D. & L. Forms/C./2118/14.

21

Instructions regarding War Diaries and Intelligence Summaries are contained in F. S. Regs., Part II, and the Staff Manual respectively. Title pages will be prepared in manuscript.

WAR DIARY
or
INTELLIGENCE SUMMARY.
(Erase heading not required.)

28TH MOBILE VETERINARY SECTION.
No.
Date.

Army Form C. 2118.

37

V/L 36

Place	Date	Hour	Summary of Events and Information	Remarks and references to Appendices
LOGEAST WOOD	1.9.18. to 3.9.18		Admitted 13 animals. Evacuated 16. discharged 1 to Unit & 1 was destroyed for Shellwds. Section moved to AVESNES-les-BAUPAME on evening of 3rd, in the course of which it was bombed on the main road to BAPAUME. No casualties occurred.	
AVESNES-les-BAPAUME.	4/9/18 to 7/9/18.		Animals picketted in trenches about 5 feet deep. Weather beautiful. Men billeted in dug-outs. admitted 15 casualties. Evacuated 5. Prepared to move on morning of 8th instant	
"	8/9/18.		Evacuated 7 to VES. discharged 1. Destroyed 2. Moved to FAVREUIL arriving there at 10 a.m. Found stables filthy & dug-outs nearly all occupied. Had stables cleaned out & got settled down. 112th Inf Bde HQ. (Rear) moved off in afternoon thus freeing dug-outs.	
FAVREUIL.	9/9/18 to 10/9/18		Admitted 12 cases. Evacuated 13. DADVS. visited Section daily. Weather very showery. Prepared to move on morning of 11/9/18.	
"	11/9/18		Evacuated two animals before move. Moved to FREMICOURT. Arrived there 11 a.m. & got settled down by 1 p.m. Admitted 15 animals today.	
FREMICOURT	12/9/18 to 16/9/18.		Weather good. Daily visits by DADVS. ADVS Corps visited Section 16/9/18. Admitted 91 animals. Evacuated 77 discharged one cured. Destroyed 2. Enemy shelled the village heavily with high explosives on 12th 13th & 14th. Bombed heavily night of 15th. Enemy plane brought down in flames (2 occupants) Terrific thunderstorm during night of 16/9/18.	

A6945/Wt. W11422/M1160 350,000 12/16 D. D. & L. Forms/C./2118/14.

Instructions regarding War Diaries and Intelligence Summaries are contained in F. S. Regs., Part II. and the Staff Manual respectively. Title pages will be prepared in manuscript.

WAR DIARY
or
INTELLIGENCE SUMMARY.
(Erase heading not required.)

23TH MOBILE VETERINARY SECTION. No. .... Date. ....

Army Form C. 2118.

Place	Date	Hour	Summary of Events and Information	Remarks and references to Appendices
FREMICOURT	17.9.18 to 20.9.18.		Admitted 47 cases for evacuation. Evacuated 62 to 5th V.E.S. 1 cured & re-issued 1 horse died of shellwounds & 2 animals were destroyed for same reason. ADVS Corps visited Section 19/9/18. DVS expected same day but did not come. Prepared to move back for Divisional Rest on 21/9/18.	
WARLENCOURT EAUCOURT	21/9/18		Left Fremicourt 9. am & arrived at WARLENCOURT - EAUCOURT 11. am. Remainder of day spent attending to sanitation, picketting arrangements, billeting & generally speaking making camp.	
WARLENCOURT EAUCOURT	22/9/18. to 29/9/18		ADVS Corps visited Section, 23/9/18 & 24/9/18. Admitted nine animals, evacuated 8 to VES. Discharged 2. One mule died from shellwounds. Two men went on leave 26/9/18. Received orders & prepared to move 29/9/18. Left WARLENCOURT 2pm 29th.	
VILLERS-AU-FLOS	29/9/18 to 30/9/18		Arrived 4.30pm settled down for night. Ready to move early on 30/9/18 to NEUVILLE.	
NEUVILLE	30/9/18.		Arrived 12.30pm. Remainder of day spent making camp etc.	

[signature] Capt AVC
O.C. 28th M.V.S.

A6945 Wt. W11422/M1160 350,000 12/16 D. D. & L. Forms/C./2118/14.

3

WAR DIARY
or
INTELLIGENCE SUMMARY.
(Erase heading not required.)

Army Form C. 2118.

28th MVS
Vol 38

Instructions regarding War Diaries and Intelligence Summaries are contained in F. S. Regs., Part II, and the Staff Manual respectively. Title pages will be prepared in manuscript.

Place	Date	Hour	Summary of Events and Information	Remarks and references to Appendices
NEUVILLE	1/10/18 to 6/10/18		Admitted 29 animals Evacuated 28 to VES. One horse died. During this period roofs were put over existing shelters for horses. A light horse was salved but was unfortunately claimed by N.Z. M.V.S. One ordinary leave on 4/10/18 (Pte Pratt) & one Special leave 6/10/18 (Dr Stewart ASC). Received orders to move on 6/10/18. Left NEUVILLE 2pm 6/10/18 & proceeded to GOUZEACOURT.	
GOUZEACOURT	6/10/18.		Arrived 4 pm. Struck camp & received two cases suffering from Shell wounds.	
"	7/10/18		Visited units 15 animals admitted	
"	8/10/18		DADVS call. improved horse lines & camp. admitted 2 casualties 1 Destroyed 17. evacuated to IV. VES.	
~~Vaucelles~~ VAUCELLES	~~9/10/18~~ 9.10.18.		Left GOUZEACOURT. and arrived VAUCELLES. at 12 PM. 9 casualties admitted & evacuated	
CHATEAU BRISEUX	10.10.18		Left for CHATEAU-BRISEUX. & camped in wood 12 animals admitted. before leaving VAUCELLES. 4 animals admitted & evacuated	
"	11.10.18.		DADVS visited Section. 13 animals evacuated 4 admitted	
"	12.10.18.		Visited Train Co. 4 animals admitted yesterday 1 died 3 evacuated Started Clipping Section Horses	

A6945 Wt. W11422/M1160 350,000 12/16 D. D. & L. Forms/C./2118/14.

Instructions regarding War Diaries and Intelligence Summaries are contained in F. S. Regs., Par. II. and the Staff Manual respectively. Title pages will be prepared in manuscript.

WAR DIARY
or
INTELLIGENCE SUMMARY.
(*Erase heading not required.*)

Army Form C. 2118.

Place	Date	Hour	Summary of Events and Information	Remarks and references to Appendices
CHATEAU-BRISEUX	13.	10.18	Received orders to move to LIGNY. after evacuating 13 animals destroying one. completed the move. & cleaned billets & camp disinfected stables	
LIGNY	"	14. 10.18.	6 Casualties admitted yesterday & same number today	
"	"	15. 10.18.	Started Divisional clipping Station. 74 animals were clipped 7 animals yesterday were evacuated & 5 today from Section	
"	"	16. 10.18.	Weather continues fair visited clipping station 3 times the G.O.C of Division also inspected same with A.M.Q.M.G. 100 horses clipped	
		17. 10.18	6 Casualties admitted visited units 112 Brigade & 4 Cos of A.S.C also clipping Station	
"	" to	18. 10.18 to 22. 10.18	During this period 26 animals were admitted to Section 27 evacuated 2 destroyed 2 Discharged. visited units & supervised Divl. Clipping Station over 500 horses clipped received orders to move to CAUDRY	
CAUDRY		23. 10.18.	Move clipping station & Section to this place weather fine. 9 animals admitted 5 evacuated. ordered to move to Beaurain.	
BEAURAIN		24. 10.18	admitted 5 animals evacuated 4 camped in open no billets obtainable	

A6945 Wt. W11422/M1160 350,000 12/16 D. D. & L. Forms/C./2118/14.

Army Form C. 2118.

Instructions regarding War Diaries and Intelligence Summaries are contained in F. S. Regs., Part II. and the Staff Manual respectively. Title pages will be prepared in manuscript.

WAR DIARY
or
INTELLIGENCE SUMMARY.
(Erase heading not required.)

Place	Date	Hour	Summary of Events and Information	Remarks and references to Appendices
BEAURAIN	25·10·18		During this period 85 casualties were admitted and 74 evacuated	
"	to		5 animals were destroyed for shell wounds + 5 discharged to	
"	31-10·18		various units. The village has been shelled almost daily	
			but particularly during the night of 29th/30th one shell exploding	
			just outside the hedge where several horses were tied fortunately doing	
			no damage.	
			Jno Hey Yates Capt AVC	
			O.C 28th M.V.S	

A6945 Wt. W11422/M1160 350,000 12/16 D. D. & L. Forms/C./2118/14.

4

Instructions regarding War Diaries and Intelligence Summaries are contained in F. S. Regs., Part II, and the Staff Manual respectively. Title pages will be prepared in manuscript.

WAR DIARY
or
INTELLIGENCE SUMMARY.
(*Erase heading not required.*)

28TH MOBILE VETERINARY SECTION.
No.
Date

Army Form C. 2118.

37

VR 39

Place	Date	Hour	Summary of Events and Information	Remarks and references to Appendices
BEAURAIN	1.11.18		Usual routine duties visited units weather fine and warm. Evacuated 8 animals to IV VES. Started revetting horse lines	
"	2.11.18		From 12.30 to 2 P.M. enemy shell vicinity one unit a heavy Battery had 9 animals killed rendered what assistance I could with Sgt Thomas A.V.C. Shot one H D with broken leg result of shell fire	
"	3.11.18		Went to SALESCHES, and arranged for place for Advanced Veterinary Aid Post, during the night heavy shelling over lines by Enemy. Office work & usual routine duties	
"	4.11.18		Established advanced V.M.S. 10 animals were admitted all with wounds result of Shelling, evacuated Eight & destroyed one	
"	5.11.18		Inspected rifles & usual routine work. 5 casualties admitted evacuated 5 destroyed one & one cured to unit.	
LOUVIGNIES	6.11.18		Weather bad heavy rains received orders to move to LOUVIGNIES admitted 3 animals withdrew advanced aid post destroyed two arrived at new camp all wet through fixed up camp & settled for night	

A6945 Wt. W11422/M1160 350,000 12/16 D. D. & L. Forms/C./2118/14.

Instructions regarding War Diaries and Intelligence Summaries are contained in F. S. Regs., Par. II, and the Staff Manual respectively. Title pages will be prepared in manuscript.

WAR DIARY
or
INTELLIGENCE SUMMARY.
(Erase heading not required.)

Army Form C. 2118.

Place	Date	Hour	Summary of Events and Information	Remarks and references to Appendices
LOUVIGNIES.	7.11.18		Weather condition on 7th bad found plenty of dead Bosche	
"		"	round village also horses. on the 8th inst weather improved	
"		"	usual routine work took charge of clipping station 13 animals	
"			captured from the enemy were sent in and 4 animals for	
"		"	various diseases & mallened & during this period 19 casualties	
"			were taken in by section. 15 were evacuated destroyed two	
"	10.11.18		& re issued 14 received orders to move & moved to CAUDRY	
CAUDRY	12.11.18		weather much improved. Started clipping station at new place	
"		"	& clipped over 100 animals. improved billets & cleaned out place inspected	
"		"	rifles & hot respirators 5 animals were admitted with various diseases to section	
"			and one evacuated	
"	13.11.18		Usual Office & routine work. weather turned very cold but fine	
			had transport painted & harness thoroughly cleaned during this period	
"		15	49 animals were admitted suffering from various diseases to section	
"			41 evacuated 5 discharged. The French people have began to arrive	
	18.11.18		back in this village and am rendering what assistance we can	

Army Form C. 2118.

Instructions regarding War Diaries and Intelligence Summaries are contained in F. S. Regs., Part II. and the Staff Manual respectively. Title pages will be prepared in manuscript.

WAR DIARY
or
INTELLIGENCE SUMMARY.
(Erase heading not required.)

Place	Date	Hour	Summary of Events and Information	Remarks and references to Appendices
CAUDRY	19-11-18		Usual routine work and office duties. Inspection of men's rifles kits and etc. 3 AVC men went sick and went to CCS also one ASC driver the later has been replaced. read various orders on Parade re, re-enlistment + ~~[illegible]~~ demobilization during this period weather conditions fairly good except on 28th inst when it rained incessantly all day. On 16th inst. the section took part in a general parade of the division before the GOC of the division 153 animals were admitted to the section during this period of which 2 were destroyed for incurable diseases and 154 animals evacuated to VI V.E.S.	28 MOBILE SECTION ARMY VETERINARY CORPS
			Jno Hy Yates Capt. O.C. 28th M.V.S.	

A6945 Wt. W11422/M1160 350,000 12/16 D. D. & L. Forms/C./2118/14.

9/12

Instructions regarding War Diaries and Intelligence Summaries are contained in F. S. Regs., Part II. and the Staff Manual respectively. Title pages will be prepared in manuscript.

WAR DIARY
or
INTELLIGENCE SUMMARY.
(Erase heading not required.)

Army Form C. 2118.

37

28 ... ARMY VETERINARY CORPS

VD 40

Place	Date	Hour	Summary of Events and Information	Remarks and references to Appendices
CAUDRY.	1-12-18		Usual section work. received orders to prepare to move and made necessary preparations. cleared out all cases to VI VES	
GOMMEGNIES.	2.12.18		moved section with D.H.Q group to this place about 21 miles arrived in the dark. and made horses and men as comfortable as possible.	
"	3-12-18		During this period weather condition bad rain fell every day. visited units usual section work, and Office	
	to		work. filled up forms for demobilization of men & answered correspondance regarding same. Save lectures on Veterinary	
"	14.12.18.		Work to Sommersets light Infantry received orders to prepare to move on 15th inst.	
Sous le BOIS	15.12.18		arrived during the afternoon. weather conditions for marching bad. one animal sent to section very lame	
	to		& sold to local butcher. usual section work.	
	17.12.18		and visited units.	

A6945 Wt. W11422/M1160 35,000 12/16 D. D. & L. Forms/C./2118/14.

Instructions regarding War Diaries and Intelligence Summaries are contained in F. S. Regs., Part II. and the Staff Manual respectively. Title pages will be prepared in manuscript.

WAR DIARY
or
INTELLIGENCE SUMMARY.
(Erase heading not required.)

Army Form C. 2118.

Place	Date	Hour	Summary of Events and Information	Remarks and references to Appendices
BINCHE.	18.12.18		Section moved to this place arriving about 3 PM. found good billets for men and section	
"	19.12.18.		Usual section duties + preparation for final move.	
GOSSELIES	20.12.18		arrived here about 4. P.M. found accommodation for horses very limited. + Section placed outside the Town however found better accommodation for horses & men in the town moved on 22nd to 57 Rue la NAMUR. during this period 61 Horses were admitted to Section for various causes 56 were evacuated to VES. 2 animals were sold for Butchery. During the month Section frequently visited by DADVS.	
			[illegible signature] Capt. RAVC. O.C. 28th MVS	

A6945 Wt. W11422/M1160 350,000 12/16 D. D. & L. Forms/C./2118/14.

9/3 37

Instructions regarding War Diaries and Intelligence Summaries are contained in F. S. Regs., Par. II, and the Staff Manual respectively. Title pages will be prepared in manuscript.

WAR DIARY
or
INTELLIGENCE SUMMARY.
(Erase heading not required.)

Army Form C. 2118.

28 Mob Vety Co

Vol 41

Place	Date	Hour	Summary of Events and Information	Remarks and references to Appendices
GOSSELIES	1.1.19		Usual section duties. Rifle inspection r.t.c. on this date. 3 animals evacuated to W.V.E.S. Appointed permanent member of board for classification of animals for demobilization and visited & classified various unit animals. Condition generally of horses and mules very good. very few of the lower class in each unit. during this period 79 animals were admitted to section for various reasons and 72 evacuated and 2 sold to butchery good prices were obtained. 1 N.C.O. from section demobilized being a pivotal man. Granted leave and propose to leave on the 16th inst. handed over section	
to	16.1.19		to D.A.D.V.S and all monies	
	17.1.19 to 31.1.19		D.A.D.V.S superintended Section, arranged Butchery transactions with Local Horse Butchers. W.V.E.S. closed 28/1/19. Found we could not evacuate anywhere, so treatment was commenced & animals returned to Units when cured. Remount Board for demobilization of Horses Classified Section animals on 25/1/19.	

Jno Hy Yates Capt
O.C. 28th M.V.S.

A6945 Wt. W11422/M1160 350,000 12/16 D. D. & L. Forms/C./2118/14.

31

Instructions regarding War Diaries and Intelligence Summaries are contained in F. S. Regs., Par. II. and the Staff Manual respectively. Title pages will be prepared in manuscript.

WAR DIARY
or
INTELLIGENCE SUMMARY.
(Erase heading not required.)

Army Form C. 2118.

Vol 42

Place	Date	Hour	Summary of Events and Information	Remarks and references to Appendices
GOSSELIES.	1/2/19.		Usual Section work. reported back from leave & took over section on 4th inst. Several changes in personal took place owing to demobilization of men. during this period kept very busy examining horses & selecting do for sales at GAMBLEU also appointed Officer in charge of divisional sales and made necessary arrangements & attended same. These sales were successful and animals made fair prices considering their low catagory. Handed over section temporary to Capt. Offord owing to the amount of work involved. A number of horses & mules were sold to local Horse butchers for food these were animals of Z class with chronic diseases & not worth treatment. The Section was	
"	28/2/19		visited by the D.A.D.V.S. daily.	
			Jno Hy Yates Capt RAVC O.C. 28th MVS	

A6945 Wt. W11422/M1160 350,000 12/16 D. D. & L. Forms/C./2118/14.

24

WAR DIARY
or
INTELLIGENCE SUMMARY.
(Erase heading not required.)

Army Form C. 2118.

34th Divl MVS
Vol 4

Instructions regarding War Diaries and Intelligence Summaries are contained in F. S. Regs., Part II. and the Staff Manual respectively. Title pages will be prepared in manuscript.

Place	Date	Hour	Summary of Events and Information	Remarks and references to Appendices
GOSSELIES	1-3-19		Sales were held of Z Surplus animals during the early part of this month and prices realized were quite good the average at the final sale for horses & mules was over 1000 Francs. Paid over all monies to field cashier and ~~[illegible]~~ prepared to reduce ~~[illegible]~~ section to cadre ~~A~~B strength.	
W			Over 50 animals were sold for butchery suffering from various diseases. Capt Offord had charge of the section during my absence at Sales. Sgt Bevan Senior Sgt who had been with section since formation was demobilized as well as others.	
			Many animals were evacuated to Advanced V. H. & usual	
	31-3-19		section work carried out.	
			Jno Hy Yates Capt RAVC	

D. D. & L., London, E.C.
(A10266) Wt W5300/P713 750,000 2/18 Sch. 52 Forms/C2118/16.

www.ingramcontent.com/pod-product-compliance
Lightning Source LLC
Chambersburg PA
CBHW081528160426
43191CB00011B/1706
* 9 7 8 1 4 7 4 5 1 8 1 9 2 *